Abbey Sage Richardson

Songs from the Old Dramatists

Abbey Sage Richardson

Songs from the Old Dramatists

ISBN/EAN: 9783337376826

Printed in Europe, USA, Canada, Australia, Japan

Cover: Foto ©Thomas Meinert / pixelio.de

More available books at **www.hansebooks.com**

Songs

FRÓM THE

OLD DRAMATISTS

COLLECTED AND EDITED BY

ABBY SAGE RICHARDSON

NEW YORK

PUBLISHED BY HURD AND HOUGHTON

Cambridge: The Riverside Press

1873

PREFACE.

A NUMBER of years ago I made for my own delectation a collection of lyrics from the works of some of the early play-writers, among which were the graceful little songs scattered through the plays of Beaumont and Fletcher, the songs from Shakespeare, and some of those especially beautiful from the works of Robert Greene and Thomas Lodge.

This collection, so small that it was contained in a pocket extract book, was so charming that it suggested to me the making of one which should be larger and more complete. I have named the volume, "Songs from the Old Dramatists," because in most cases I have taken them intact from the body of some old English drama, or else I have found them among the fugitive poems of some of the dramatic poets, who were in the habit of interspersing their plays with songs. The greater part of these in this volume have, at some time, been set to music; and many of them have in their day been fashionable madrigals. Now they are quaint memorials of an age long since gone by.

I think we shall like these all the more, because our great poets of this present day write no songs. Since the time of Charles II., there have been hardly any

English poets who were singers. A few melodies from
Tom Moore and Barry Cornwall, two or three from
Shelley and Tennyson, are about all we could add to
those of Shakespeare's day. We are too serious nowa-
days to sing like the birds, as the early singers sang in
the morning of poesy.

I know the verses in this volume so much by heart,
and I am so fond of them, that I feel almost as if I had
a part in the making of them. If there is any one over
whom they exercise a like charm, I commend this book
to his gentle keeping, and warrant it a rich treasure-
house of pure English song.

A. S. R.

CONTENTS.

———♦———

The Songs were collected and the notes prepared by A. S. Richardson; the drawings were made by J. La Farge; the ornamental designs and vignette by S. L. Smith.

PASTORAL SONGS

SONGS OF NATURE.

———◆———

BIRD SONG.

FROM "ALEXANDER AND CAMPASPE."

WHAT bird so sings, yet does so wail?
  O, 'tis the ravished nightingale;
"Jug, jug — jug, jug — tereu," she cries,
  And still her woes at midnight rise.

Brave prick-song! who is't now we hear?
  None but the lark so shrill and clear;
Now at heaven's gates she claps her wings,
  The morn not waking till she sings.

Hark, hark! with what a pretty throat,
  Poor Robin Redbreast tunes his note!
Hark! how the jolly cuckoos sing
  "Cuckoo" — to welcome in the spring.

JOHN LYLY.

I

THE PRAISE OF PHILIP SPARROW.

OF all the birds that I do know,
  Philip, my sparrow, hath no peer,
For sit she high, or lie she low,
  Be she far off, or be she near,
There is no bird so fair and fine,
Nor yet so fresh as this of mine.

Come in a morning merrily,
  When Philip has been lately fed;
Or in an evening soberly,
  When Philip list to go to bed;
It is a heaven to hear my Phip,
How she can chirp with cherry lip.

Wherefore I sing and ever shall,
  To praise as I have often proved,
There is no bird amongst them all,
  So worthy for to be beloved.
Let others praise what birds they will,
Sweet Philip shall be my bird still.

GEORGE GASCOIGNE.

SPRING AND SUMMER.

FROM "WILL SOMER'S LAST WILL AND TESTAMENT."

I.

SPRING.

SPRING, the sweet spring, is the year's pleasant king :
Then blooms each thing, then maids dance in ring,
Cold doth not sting, the pretty birds do sing,
Cuckoo, jug, jug, pu-we, to-witta-woo.

The palm and may make country houses gay,
Lambs frisk and play, the shepherds pipe all day,
And, hear we aye, birds tune their pretty lay,
Cuckoo, jug, jug, pu-we, to-witta-woo.

The fields breathe sweet, the daisies kiss our feet,
Young lovers meet, old wives a sunning sit ;
In every street, these tunes our ears do greet,
Cuckoo, jug, jug, pu-we, to-witta-woo.
            Spring, the sweet spring.

II.

SUMMER.

Fair summer droops, droop men and beast therefore
So fair a summer look for never more ;

All good things vanish less than in a day,
Peace, plenty, pleasure, suddenly decay.
    Go not yet away, bright soul of the sad year,
    The earth is hell when thou leav'st to appear.

What, shall these flowers that decked thy garland
    erst,
Upon thy grave be wastefully dispersed?
O trees, consume your sap in sorrow's source,
Streams, turn to tears your tributary course,
    Go not yet away, bright soul of the sad year,
    The earth is hell when thou leav'st to appear.

Thomas Nash.

THE SEASONS.

FROM "LOVE'S LABOR LOST."

I.

SPRING.

When daisies pied, and violets blue,
    And lady-smocks all silver white,
And cuckoo-buds of yellow hue,
    Do paint the meadows with delight,
The cuckoo then, on every tree
Mocks married men: for thus sings he,
      Cuckoo;
Cuckoo, Cuckoo, — O word of fear,
Unpleasing to a married ear!

When shepherds pipe on oaten straws,
    And merry larks are ploughman's clocks;
When turtles tread, and rooks and daws,
    And maidens bleach their summer smocks,
The cuckoo then, on every tree
Mocks married men: for thus sings he,
        Cuckoo;
Cuckoo, cuckoo,— O word of fear,
Unpleasing to the married ear!

II.

WINTER.

When icicles hang by the wall,
    And Dick the shepherd blows his nail,
And Tom bears logs into the hall,
    And milk comes frozen home in pail;
When blood is nipped, and ways be foul,
Then nightly sings the staring owl,
        To-who;
Tu-whit, tu-who, a merry note,
While greasy Joan doth keel the pot.

When all aloud the wind doth blow,
    And coughing drowns the parson's saw,
And birds sit brooding in the snow,
    And Marian's nose looks red and raw;

When roasted crabs hiss in the bowl,
Then nightly sings the staring owl,
      To-who ;
To-whit, to-who, a merry note,
While greasy Joan doth keel the pot.
                WILLIAM SHAKESPEARE.

PHILLIDA AND CORYDON.

In the merry month of May,
In a morn by break of day,
Forth I walked by the wood-side,
When as May was in his pride ;
There I spièd all alone,
Phillida and Corydon.
Much ado there was, God wot ;
He would love, and she would not.
She said, "Never man was true ; "
He said, "None was false to you : "
He said he had loved her long ;
She said, Love should have no wrong.
Coridon would kiss her then,
She said, Maids must kiss no men,
Till they did for good and all.
Then she made the shepherd call
All the heavens to witness truth
Never loved a truer youth.
Thus with many a pretty oath,

Yea and nay, and faith and troth,
Such as silly shepherds use,
When they still will love abuse,
Love, which has been long deluded,
Was with kisses sweet concluded ;
And Phillida, with garlands gay,
Was made the lady of the May.

NICHOLAS BRETON.

HYMNS TO PAN.

FROM "PAN'S ANNIVERSARY, A MASQUE."

HYMN I.

(Sung by Nymphs strewing flowers.)

THUS, thus begin the yearly rites,
Are due to Pan on these bright nights ;
His morn now riseth, and invites
To sports, to dances, and delights ;
  All envious and profane away,
  This is the shepherd's holiday.

Strew, strew the glad and smiling ground
With every flower, yet not confound
The primrose drop, the spring's own spouse,
Bright day's eyes and the lips of cows,
  The garden star, the queen of May,
  The rose, to crown the holiday.

Drop, drop your violets, change your hues,
Now red, now pale, as lovers use ;
And in your death go out as well,
As when you lived unto the smell ;
   That from your odor all may say,
   This is the shepherd's holiday.

HYMN II.

Of Pan we sing, the best of singers, Pan,
   That taught us swains how first to tune our lay,
And on the pipe more airs than Phœbus can.
   Hear, O you groves, and hills resound his praise.

Of Pan we sing, the best of leaders, Pan,
   That leads the Naiads and the Dryads forth,
And to their dances more than Hermes can.
   Hear, O you groves, and hills resound his worth.

Of Pan we sing, the best of hunters, Pan,
   That drives the hart to seek unusèd ways,
And in the chase more than Sylvanus can.
   Hear, O you groves, and hills resound his praise.

Of Pan we sing, the best of shepherds, Pan,
   That keeps our flocks and herds, and both leads
      forth
To better pastures than great Pales can.
   Hear, O you groves, and hills resound his worth.

And while his power and praises thus we sing,
The valleys let rebound, and all the rivers ring.

HYMN III.

If yet, if yet
Pan's orgies you will further fit,
See where the silver-footed fays do sit,
The nymphs of wood and water,
Each tree's and fountain's daughter.
Go take them forth, it will be good,
To see them wave it like a wood,
And others mind it like a flood,
In springs,
And rings,
Till the applause it brings,
Wakes Echo from her seat,
The closes to repeat.
Echo. The closes to repeat.
Echo, the truest oracle on ground,
Though nothing but a sound,
Echo. Though nothing but a sound.
Beloved of Pan, the valley's queen,
Echo. The valley's queen,
And often heard, though never seen,
Echo. Though never seen.

BEN JONSON.

SHEPHERD'S SONG.

WE that have known no greater state
Than this we live in, praise our fate,
For courtly silks in cares are spent,
When country's russet breeds content.

The power of sceptres we admire,
But sheep-crooks for our use desire;
Simple and low is our condition,
For here with us is no ambition.

We with the sun our flocks unfold,
Whose rising makes their fleeces gold;
Our music from the birds we borrow,
They bidding us, we them, good-morrow.

Our habits are but coarse and plain,
Yet 'they defend from wind and rain,
As warm too, in an equal eye,
As those bestained in scarlet dye.

The shepherd with his homespun lass,
As many merry hours doth pass,
As courtiers with their costly girls,
Though richly decked in gold and pearls.

                                    THOMAS HEYWOOD.

ODE TO THE COUNTRY.

Come, spur away,
I have no patience for a longer stay,
   But must go down,
   And leave the chargeable noise of this great town.
I will the country see,
Where old Simplicity,
   Though hid in gray,
   Doth look more gay
Than Foppery, in plush and scarlet clad.
   Farewell, you city wits, that are
   Almost at civil war!
'Tis time that I grow wise, when all the world goes
   mad.

More of my days,
I will not spend to gain an idiot's praise;
   Or to make sport
   For some slight pigmy of the inns of court.
Then, worthy Stafford, say,
How shall we spend the day,
   With what delights
   Shorten the nights,
When from this tumult we are got secure?
   Where Mirth with all her freedom goes,
   Yet shall no finger lose,
Where every word is thought, and every thought is
   pure.

There from the tree
We'll cherries pluck, and pick the strawberry;
    And every day
    Go see the wholesome country girls make hay;
Whose brown hath lovelier grace,
Than any painted face,
    That I do know
    Hyde Park can show.
Where I had rather. gain a kiss, than meet
    (Though some of them in greater state
    Might court my love with plate)
The beauties of the Cheap, and wives of Lombard
    Street.

    But think upon
Some other pleasures, these to me are none;
    Why do I prate
    Of women, that are things against my fate?
I never mean to wed,
That torture to my bed;
    My Muse is she
    My love shall be;
Let clowns get wealth and heirs! when I am gone,
    And that great bugbear, grisly Death,
    Shall take this idle breath,
If I a poem leave, that poem is my son.

    Of this no more,
We'll rather taste the bright Pomona's store,

No fruit shall 'scape
Our palate, from the damson to the grape;
Then full, we'll seek a shade,
And hear what music's made;
How Philomel
Her tale doth tell,
And how the other birds do fill the choir;
The thrush and blackbird lend their throats,
Warbling melodious notes.
We will all sports enjoy, which others but desire.

Ours is the sky
Where at what fowl we please, our hawk shall fly;
Nor will we spare
To hunt the crafty fox, or timorous hare,
But let our hounds run loose,
In any ground they choose:
The buck shall fall,
The stag and all;
Our pleasures must from their own warrants be,
For to my Muse, if not to me,
I'm sure all game is free;
Heaven, earth, are all but parts of her great royalty.

And when we mean
To taste of Bacchus' blessings now and then
And drink by stealth
A cup or two to noble Barkley's health,

I'll take my pipe and try
The Phrygian melody,
 Which he that hears
 Lets through his ears
A madness to distemper all the brain ;
 Then I another pipe will take
 And Doric music make,
To civilize with graver notes our wits again.

Thomas Randolph.

SHEPHERD'S SONGS TO PAN.

FROM " THE FAITHFUL SHEPHERDESS."

I.

Sing his praises that doth keep
 Our flocks from harm,
Pan, the father of our sheep ;
 And, arm in arm,
Tread we softly in a round,
Whilst the hollow neighboring ground
Fills the music with her sound.

Pan, O great god Pan, to thee
 Thus do we sing !
Thou that keep'st us chaste and free
 As the young spring ;
Ever be thy praises spoke,

From that place the Morn is broke,
To that place Day doth unyoke.

II.

All ye woods, and trees, and bowers,
All ye virtues and ye powers,
That inhabit in the lakes,
In the pleasant springs or brakes,
　　　Move your feet
　　　　　To our sound,
　　　Whilst we greet
　　　　　All the ground
With his honor and his name,
That defends our flocks from blame.

He is great, and he is just,
He is ever good, and must
Thus be honored. Daffodillies,
Roses, pinks, and lovèd lilies,
　　　Let us fling,
　　　Whilst we sing,
　　　Ever holy,
　　　Ever holy,
Ever honored, ever young!
Thus great Pan is ever sung.
　　　　　BEAUMONT AND FLETCHER.

HARVEST HOME.

FROM "THE SUN'S DARLING."

HAYMAKERS, rakers, reapers, and mowers,
  Wait on your summer queen ;
Dress with musk-roses her eglantine bowers,
  Daffodils strew the green ;
    Sing, dance, and play,
    'Tis holyday ;
  The sun doth bravely shine
  On our ears of corn ;
    Rich as a pearl,
    Comes every girl,
  This is mine, this is mine, this is mine ;
  Let us die ere away they be bourne.

Bow to the sun, to our queen, and that fair one
  Come to behold our sports ;
Each bonny lass here is counted a rare one,
  As those in prince's courts.
    These and we,
    With country glee,
  Will teach the woods to resound,
  And the hills with echoes hollow ;
    Skipping lambs,
    Their bleating dams,
  'Mongst kids shall trip it round :
  For joys, thus our lasses we follow.

Wind, jolly huntsmen, your neat bugles shrilly,
    Hounds, make a lusty cry ;
Spring up, you falconers, the partridges freely,
    Then let you brave hawks fly.
      Horses amain
      Over ridge, over plain,
    The dogs have the stag in chase ;
    'Tis a sport to content a king.
      So ho ! ho ! through the skies
      How the proud bird flies,
And swooping, kills with a grace !
Now the deer falls ; hark ! how they ring.

JOHN FORD.

LESBIA AND HER SPARROW.

    TELL me not of joy ! there 's none,
    Now my little sparrow 's gone ;
      He, just as you,
      Would toy and woo,
    He would chirp and flatter me,
      He would hang the wing awhile,
      Till at length he saw me smile —
    Lord ! how sullen he would be.

    He would catch a crumb, and then
    Sporting, let it go again ;

2

He from my lip
Would moisture sip ;
He would from my trencher feed ;
Then would hop, and then would run,
And cry Philip when he'd done ;
O ! whose heart can choose but bleed.
O ! how eager would he fight,
And ne'er hurt though he did bite,
No morn did pass
But on my glass
He would sit, and mark, and do
What I did, now ruffle all
His feathers o'er, now let them fall,
And then straightway sleek them too.

Whence will Cupid get his darts
Feathered now, to pierce our hearts ?
A wound, he may,
Not love, convey,
Now this faithful bird is gone.
O ! let mournful turtles join
With loving redbreasts, and combine
To sing dirges o'er his stone.

WILLIAM CARTWRIGHT.

SPRING.

FROM "THE TRUE TROJANS."

At the spring,
Birds do sing,
Now with high,
Then low cry,
   Chorus. He's no bard that cannot sing
            The praises of the flowery spring.

Flat, acute,
And salute
The sun, born
Every morn.

Flora queen,
All in green,
Doth delight
To paint white,
   Chorus. He's no bard, etc.

And to spread,
Cruel red,
With a blue,
Color true.

Woods renew
Hunter's hue,
Shepherds gray,
Crowned with bay,
   Chorus. He's no bard, etc.

With his pipe
Care doth wipe,
Till he dream
By the stream.

Faithful loves,
Turtle doves,
Sit and bill
On a hill.
   Chorus. He's no bard, etc.

Country swains,
On the plains,
Run and leap,
Turn and skip.

Pan doth play
Care away :
Fairies small,
Two foot tall,
 Chorus. He's no bard, etc.

With caps red,
On their head,
Dance around
On the ground.

Phillis bright,
All in white,
With neck fair,
Yellow hair,
 Chorus. He's no bard that cannot sing
   The praises of the flowery spring.

Rocks doth move
With her love,
And make mild
Tigers wild.

JASPER FISHER.

LABORER'S SONG.

FROM "LONDON'S TRIUMPH, A MASQUE."

WHO can boast a happiness
 More securely safe than we ?
Since our harmless thoughts we dress
 In a pure simplicity ;
And chaste nature doth dispense
Here, her beauty's innocence.

Envy is a stranger here,
 Blest content our bowls doth crown ;
Let such slave themselves to fear,
 On whose guilt the judge doth frown,

We from evil actions are
Free as uncorrupted air.

With the turtles whisper love,
  With the birds do practice mirth,
With our harmless sheep we move,
  And receive our food from earth,
Nor do we disdain to be
Clothed with the lamb's livery.

JOHN TATHAM.

THE NIGHTINGALE.

O NIGHTINGALE, that on yon bloomy spray
  Warblest at eve, when all the woods are still,
  Thou with fresh hope the lover's heart dost fill,
While the jolly hours lead on propitious May.

Thy liquid notes that close the eye of day,
  First heard before the shallow cuckoo's bill,
  Portend success in love ; O, if Jove's will
Have linked that amorous power to thy soft lay.

Now timely sing, ere the rude bird of hate
  Foretell my hopeless doom in some grove nigh ;
As thou from year to year hast sung too late
  For my relief, yet hadst no reason why.

Whether the Muse, or Love call thee his mate,
Both them I serve, and of their train am I.

JOHN MILTON.

ARCADES.

SONGS OF SHEPHERDS AND NYMPHS.

FROM ARCADES ; A MASQUE, REPRESENTED BEFORE THE COUNTESS OF
DERBY.

SONG I.

LOOK, Nymphs and Shepherds, look,
What sudden blaze of majesty
Is that which we from hence descry?
Too divine to be mistook;
This, this is she
To whom our vows and wishes tend;
Here, our solemn search hath end.

Fame, that her high worth to raise,
Seemed erst so lavish and profuse,
We may justly now accuse
Of detraction from her praise:
Less than half we find expressed,
Envy bid conceal the rest.

Mark what radiant state she spreads
In circle round her shining throne,

Shooting her beams like silver threads ;
 This, this is she alone,
  Sitting like a goddess bright
  In the centre of the light.

(*The Genius of the Wood appears.*)

Genius. Stay, gentle swains, for though in this dis-
 guise
I see bright honor sparkle through your eyes ;
Of famous Arcady ye are, and sprung
Of that renownèd flood, so often sung,
Divine Alphéus, who by secret sluice
Stole under seas to meet his Arethuse :
And ye, the breathing roses of the wood,
Fair silver-buskined Nymphs, as great and good,
I know this quest of yours, and free intent
Was in all honor and devotion meant
To the great mistress of yon princely shrine,
Whom with low reverence I adore as mine,
And with all helpful service will comply
To further this night's glad solemnity ;
And lead ye where ye may more near behold ;
What shallow-searching fame hath left untold
Which I full oft amidst these shades alone
Have sat to wonder at, and gaze upon :
For know, by lot from Jove I am the power
Of this fair wood, and live in oaken bower
To nurse the saplings tall, and curl the grove

With ringlets quaint, and wanton winding wove ;
And all my plants I save from nightly ill
Of noisome winds and blasting vapors chill :
And from the boughs brush off the evil dew,
And heal the harms of thwarting thunder blue,
Or what the cross, dire-looking planet smites,
Or hurtful worm with cankered venom bites.
When evening gray doth rise, I fetch my round
Over the mount and all this hallowed ground,
And early, ere the odorous breath of morn
Awakes the slumbering leaves, or tasseled horn
Shakes the high thicket, haste I all about,
Number my ranks, and visit every sprout
With puissant words, and murmurs made to bless ;
But else, in deep of night when drowsiness
Hath locked up mortal sense, then listen I
To the celestial Sirens' harmony,
That sit upon the vine infolded spheres,
And sing to those that hold the vital shears,
And turn the adamantine spindle round,
On which the fate of gods and men is wound.
Such sweet compulsion doth in music lie,
To lull the daughters of Necessity,
And keep unsteady Nature to her law,
And the low world in measured motion draw
After the heavenly tune, which none can hear
Of human mould, with gross unpurged ear ;
And yet such music worthiest were to blaze

The peerless height of her immòrtal praise,
Whose lustre leads us, and for her most fit,
If my inferior hand, or voice could hit
Inimitable sounds; yet as we go,
Whate'er the skill of lesser gods can show,
I will assay, her worth to celebrate,
And so attend ye toward her glittering state;
Where ye may all that are of noble stem
Approach, and kiss her sacred vesture's hem.

SONG II.

O'er the smooth enameled green,
Where no print of step hath been,
　　Follow me as I sing,
　　And touch the warbled string.
Under the shady roof
Of branching elm, star-proof.
　　Follow me,
I will bring you where she sits,
Clad in splendor as befits
　　Her deity.
Such a rural queen
All Arcadia hath not seen.

SONG III.

Nymphs and Shepherds, dance no more
　　By sandy Ladon's lilied banks;
'On old Lycæus or Cyllene hoar
　　Trip no more in twilight ranks;

Though Erymanth your loss deplore,
　A better soil shall give ye thanks.
From the stony Mænalus
Bring your flocks, and live with us,
Here ye shall have greater grace
To serve the Lady of this place.
Though Syrinx your Pan's mistress were,
Yet Syrinx well might wait on her.
　Such a rural queen
All Arcadia hath not seen.

JOHN MILTON.

SONGS.

FROM "THE MERRY BEGGARS."

I.

FROM hunger and cold who lives more free,
　Or who more richly clad than we?
Our bellies are full, our flesh is warm,
　And against pride, our rags are a charm;
Enough is our feast, and for to-morrow,
Let rich men care, we feel no sorrow;
　No sorrow, no sorrow, no sorrow, no sorrow,
　Let rich men care, we feel no sorrow.

Each city, each town, and every village,
　Affords us either an alms or pillage;

And if the weather be cold and raw,
   Then in a barn we tumble in straw,
If warm and fair, by yeacock and naycock,
   The fields will afford us a hedge or a haycock,
     A haycock, haycock, a haycock, a haycock,
     The fields will afford us a hedge or a haycock.

II.

   Come, come away, the spring,
   By every bird that can but sing,
   Or chirp a note, doth now write
   Us forth, to taste of his delight,
   In field, in grove, on hill, in dale,
   But above all, the nightingale,
   Who in her sweetness strives t'outdo
   The loudness of the hoarse cuckoo.
     Cuckoo, cries he ; jug, jug, jug, sings she,
     From bush to bush, from tree to tree :
     Why in one place then tarry we ?

   Come away, why do we stay ?
   We have no debt or rent to pay
   No bargains nor accounts to make
   Nor land, nor lease, to let or take,
   Or if we had should that remore us,
   Whén all the world's our own before us?

And where we pass, and make resort,
It is our kingdom, and our court.
　　Cuckoo, cries he ; jug, jug, jug, sings she,
　　From bush to bush, from tree to tree ;
　　Why in one place then tarry we?

RICHARD BROME.

LOVE-SONGS,

INCLUDING

SERENADES AND EPITHALAMIUMS.

————◆————

TO SYLVIA.

FROM "TWO GENTLEMEN OF VERONA."

WHO is Sylvia? What is she,
   That all our swains commend her?
Holy, fair, and wise is she;
   The heavens such grace did lend her,
That she might admired be.

Is she kind as she is fair,—
   For beauty lives with kindness?—
Love doth to her eyes repair
   To help him of his blindness;
And, being helped, inhabits there.

Then to Sylvia let us sing,
    That Sylvia is excelling;
She excels each mortal thing,
    Upon the dull earth dwelling;
To her let us garlands bring.

SHAKESPEARE.

TO IMOGEN.

FROM "CYMBELINE."

Hark! hark! the lark at heavens' gate sings,
    And Phœbus 'gins arise,
His steeds to water at those springs
    On chaliced flowers that lies;
And winking Mary-buds begin
    To ope their pretty eyes:
With everything that pretty bin,
    My lady sweet, arise;
        Arise, arise!

SHAKESPEARE.

SERENADE.

FROM "THE SPANISH CURATE."

DEAREST, do not you delay me,
    Since thou know'st I must be gone;
Wind and tide, 'tis thought, doth stay me,
    But 'tis wind that must be blown
From that breath, whose native smell
Indian odors doth excel.

O, then speak, thou fairest fair,
  Kill not him that vows to serve thee ;
But perfume this neighboring air,
  Else dull silence sure will starve me ;
'Tis a word that 's quickly spoken
Which, being restrained, a heart is broken.

BEAUMONT AND FLETCHER.

SERENADE.

TO THE QUEEN IN PRISON.

FROM "THE FALSE ONE."

LOOK out, bright eyes, and bless the air ;
Even in shadows you are fair.
Shut up beauty is like fire
That breaks out clearer still, and higher.

Though your body be confined,
  And soft love a prisoner bound,
Yet the beauty of your mind
  Neither check nor chain hath found.
Look out nobly then, and dare
Even the fetters that you wear.

BEAUMONT AND FLETCHER.

TO MY MISTRESS' EYES.

FROM " WOMEN PLEASED."

O, FAIR sweet face, O, eyes celestial bright,
Twin stars in heaven, that now adorn the night !
O, fruitful lips, where cherries ever grow,
And damask cheeks, where all sweet beauties blow !
O thou from head to foot divinely fair !
Cupid's most cunning net 's made of that hair,
And, as he weaves himself for curious eyes,
" O me, O me, I'm caught myself ! " he cries :
Sweet rest about thee, sweet and golden sleep,
Soft peaceful thoughts, your hourly watches keep,
Whilst I in wonder sing this sacrifice
To beauty sacred, and those angel eyes.

                               BEAUMONT AND FLETCHER.

WAKE, GENTLY WAKE.

FROM " WIT AT SEVERAL WEAPONS."

FAIN would I wake you sweet, but fear
I should invite you to worse cheer ;
In your dreams you cannot fare
Meaner than music, or compare ;
None of your slumbers are compiled
Under the pleasures makes a child ;
Your day-delights, so well compact,
That what you think turns all to act.

I'd wish my life no better play,
Your dream by night, your thought by day.
        Wake, gently wake,
Part softly from your dreams,
        The morning flies,
        To your fair eyes,
To take her special beams.

BEAUMONT AND FLETCHER.

SERENADE.

FROM "AMENDS FOR LADIES."

RISE, lady mistress, rise!
    The night has tedious been,
No sleep has fallen upon my eyes,
    Nor slumber made me sin:
Is she not a saint then, say,
Thought of whom keeps sin away?

Rise, madam, rise, and give me light,
    Whom darkness still will cover,
And ignorance, darker than night,
    Till thou smile on thy lover:
All want day till thy beauty rise
For the gray morn breaks from thine eyes.

NATHANIEL FIELD.

3

SONG.

UNCLOSE those eyelids, and outshine
  The brightness of the breaking day!
The light they cover is divine,
  Why should it fade so soon away?
Stars vanish so, and day appears,
The sun 's so drowned in the morning's tears.

O, let not sadness cloud that beauty,
  Which if you lose you'll ne'er recover:
It is not love's, but sorrow's duty,
  To die so soon for a dead lover.
Banish! O banish grief! and then
Our joys will bring our hopes again.
HENRY GLAPTHORNE.

MORNING.

THE lark now leaves his watery nest,
  And climbing, shakes his dewy wings,
He takes this window for the east,
  And to implore your light he sings.
Awake! awake! the morn will never rise
Till she can dress her beauty at your eyes.

The merchant bows unto the seaman's star,
  The ploughman from the sun his season takes;

But still the lover wonders what they are,
    Who look for day before his mistress wakes.
Awake! awake! break through your veils of lawn!
Then draw your curtains and begin the dawn.

SIR WILLIAM DAVENANT.

CUPID'S CURSE.

FROM "THE ARRAIGNMENT OF PARIS."

(*Œnone and Paris sing.*)

ŒNONE.

FAIR, and fair, and twice so fair,
    As fair as any may be ;
The fairest shepherd on our green,
    A love for any lady.

PARIS.

Fair, and fair, and twice so fair,
    As fair as any may be ;
Thy love is fair for thee alone,
    And for no other lady.

ŒNONE.

My love is fair, my love is gay,
And fresh as been the flowers in May,
And of my love the roundelay,
    The merry, merry, merry roundelay
        Concludes with Cupid's curse ;

They that do change old love for new,
  Pray gods they change for worse.

ŒNONE.

Fair, and fair, and twice so fair,
  As fair as any may be;
The fairest shepherd on our green,
  A love for any lady.

PARIS.

Fair, and fair, and twice so fair,
  As fair as any may be;
Thy love is fair for thee alone,
  And for no other lady.

ŒNONE.

My love can pipe, my love can sing,
My love can many a pretty thing,
And of his lovely praises ring
My merry, merry, merry roundelays,
  Amen to Cupid's curse;
They that do change old love for new,
  Pray gods they change for worse.

GEORGE PEELE.

CUPID AND CAMPASPE.

FROM "ALEXANDER AND CAMPASPE."

(*Apelles sings at his easel.*)

CUPID and my Campaspe played
At cards for kisses ; Cupid paid.
He staked his quiver, bow, and arrows,
His mother's doves, and team of sparrows ;
Loses them too, then down he throws
The coral of his lip, the rose
Growing on 's cheek (but none knows how) ;
With these, the crystal of his brow,
And then, the dimple in his chin ;
All these did my Campaspe win.
At last he set her both his eyes,
She won, and Cupid blind did rise.
O Love ! has she done this to thee ?
What shall, alas ! become of me ?

JOHN LYLY.

CUPID'S ARRAIGNMENT.

FROM "GALATHEA."

O YES ! O yes ! if any maid
Whom leering Cupid has betrayed
To frowns of spite, to eyes of scorn ;
And would in madness, now see· torn
The boy in pieces ; let her come
Hither, and lay on him her doom.

O yes! O yes! has any lost
A heart, which many a sigh hath cost?
Is any cozened of a tear,
Which, as a pearl disdain doth wear?
Here stands the thief; let her but come
Hither, and lay on him her doom.

Is any one undone by fire,
And turned to ashes by desire;
Did ever any lady weep,
Being cheated of her golden sleep,
Stol'n by sick thoughts? the pirate's found,
And in her tears he shall be drowned.

Read his indictment, let him hear
What he's to trust to. Boy, give ear!

JOHN LYLY.

ARROWS FOR LOVE.

FROM "SAPPHO AND PHAON."

(*Vulcan singing at the forge.*)

My shag-hair Cyclops, come, let's ply
The Lamnian hammers lustily;
    By my wife's sparrows,
    I wear these arrows;
    I shall singing fly
    Through many a wanton's eye.

These headed are with golden blisses,
These silver ones feathered with kisses,
    But this of lead
    Strikes a clown dead,
    When in a dance
    He falls in a trance,
To see his black-browed lass not buss him,
And then whines out for death t'untruss him.
  So! so! our work being done, let's play,
  Holiday! boys, cry holiday!

JOHN LYLY.

MYRA.

I, WITH whose colors Myra drest her head,
  I that wore poises of her own hands' making,
I, that mine own name in the cambric read,
  By Myra finely wrought ere I was waking.
    Must I look on, in hope time coming may
    With change bring back my turn again to play?

I, that on Sunday at the church-stile found
  A garland sweet with true-love-knots in flowers,
Which I to wear about mine arms was bound,
  That each of us might know that all was ours.
    Must I now lead an idle life in wishes,
    And follow Cupid for his loaves and fishes?

I, that did wear the ring her mother left,
  I, for whose love she gloried to be blamed,
I, with whose eyes her eyes committed theft,
  I, who did make her blush when I was named ;
    Must I lose ring, flowers, blush, theft, and go
      naked,
    Watching with sighs till dead love be awakèd.

FULKE GREVILLE (LORD BROOKE).

TO HER EYES.

FROM " CŒLICA."

Yon little stars that live in skies
  And glory in Apollo's glory,
In whose aspect conjoined lies
  The heaven's will, and nature's story ;
Joy to be likened to those eyes,
  Which eyes make all eyes glad or sorry.
    For when you place the thought above,
    These overrule your force by love.

FULKE GREVILLE (LORD BROOKE).

ROSALIND'S MADRIGAL.

FROM " ROSALIND ; " EUPHUES' " GOLDEN LEGACY."

Love in my bosom like a bee
  Doth suck his sweet,
Now with his wings he plays with me,
  Now with his feet.

Within mine eyes he makes his nest,
His bed, amid my tender breast,
My kisses are his daily feast,
And yet, he robs me of my rest, —
    Ah! wanton, will ye?

And if I sleep, then percheth he
        With pretty flight,
And makes his pillow of my knee
        The livelong night.
Strike I my lute, he tunes the string,
He music plays, if so I sing,
He lends me every lovely thing;
Yet cruel he, my heart doth sting, —
        Whist, wanton, will ye?

Else I with roses every day
        Will whip you hence;
And bind you when you long to play,
        For your offense.
I'll shut mine eyes to keep you in,
I'll make you fast it for your sin,
I'll count your power not worth a pin, —
Alas! what hereby shall I win,
        If he gainsay me?

What if I beat the wanton boy
        With many a rod?

He will repay me with annoy,
    Because a god.
Then sit thou softly on my knee,
And let thy bower my bosom be,
Lurk in mine eyes, I like of thee,
O Cupid, so thou pity me,
    Spare not, but play thee.

THOMAS LODGE.

ROSALIND'S DESCRIPTION.

FROM THE SAME.

LIKE to the clear in highest sphere,
    Where all imperial glory shines,
Of self-same color is her hair,
    Whether unfolded, or entwined:
      Heigho, fair Rosalind!

Her eyes are sapphires set in snow,
    Resembling heaven by every wink;
The gods do fear when as they glow,
    And I do tremble when I think
      Heigho, would she were mine!
Her cheeks are like the blushing cloud,
    That beautifies Aurora's face,
Or like the silver, crimson shroud,
    That Phœbe's smiling looks doth grace:
      Heigho, fair Rosalind!

Her lips are like two budded roses,
  Whom ranks of lilies neighbor nigh,
Within which bound she balm incloses
  Apt to entice a Deity:
    Heigho, would she were mine!
Her neck like to a stately tower,
  Where Love himself imprisoned lies,
To watch for glances every hour,
  From her divine and sacred eyes:
    Heigho, fair Rosalind!

Her paps are centres of delight,
  Her breasts are orbs of heavenly frame
Where nature moulds the dew of light,
  To feed Perfection with the same:
    Heigho, would she were mine!
With orient pearl, with ruby red,
  With marble white, and sapphire blue,
Her body every way is fed,
  Yet soft in touch, and sweet in view:
    Heigho, fair Rosalind!

Nature herself her shape admires,
  The gods are wounded in her sight,
And Love forsakes his heavenly fires,
  And at her eyes his brand doth light:
    Heigho, would she were mine!

Then muse not, nymphs, though I bemoan
The absence of fair Rosalind,
Since for her fair, there is fairer none;
Nor for her virtues so divine;
Heigho, fair Rosalind!
Heigho, my heart, would God that she were mine.

THOMAS LODGE.

MONTANE'S PRAISE OF FAIR PHŒBE.

PHŒBÈ sat,
Sweet she sate,
Sweet sate Phœbe when I saw her;
White her brow,
Coy her eye,
Brow and eye, how much you please me;
Words I spent,
Sighs I sent,
Sighs and words could never draw her;
O, my love,
Thou art lost,
Since no sight could ever ease thee.

Phœbe sate
By a fount,
Sitting by a fount I spied her,
Sweet her touch,
Rare her voice,

Touch and voice, what may distain thee?
As she sung
I did sigh,
　　And by sighs while that I tried her;
O, mine eyes,
You did lose
　　Her first sight, which want did pain you.

Phœbe's flocks,
White as wool,
　　Yet were Phœbe's locks more whiter;
Phœbe's eyes,
Dove-like mild,
　　Dove-like eyes, both mild and cruel.
Montane swears
In your lamps,
　　He will die for to delight her.
Phœbe yield,
Or I die;
　　Shall true hearts be fancy's fuel?

　　　　　　　　　　　THOMAS LODGE.

.

THE DECEITFUL MISTRESS.

Now I find thy looks were feigned,
Quickly lost, and quickly gained;
Soft thy skin like wool of weathers,
Heart unstable, light as feathers,

Tongue untrusty, subtle-sighted,
Wanton will, with change delighted.
    Siren pleasant, foe to reason,
    Cupid plague thee for this treason,

Of thine eyes I made my mirror,
From thy beauty came mine error;
All thy words I counted witty,
All thy smiles I deemèd pity;
Thy false tears, that me aggrieved,
First of all, my heart deceived.
    Siren pleasant, foe to reason,
    Cupid plague thee for this treason!

Feigned acceptance, when I asked,
Lovely words, with cunning masked,
Holy vows but heart unholy;
Wretched man! my trust was folly!
Lily-white, and pretty winking,
Solemn vows, but sorry thinking.
    Siren pleasant, foe to reason,
    Cupid plague thee for this treason!

Now I see, O, seemly cruel,
O, thus warm them at my fuel,
Wit shall guide me in this durance,
Since in love is no assurance;

Change thy pasture, take thy pleasure,
Beauty is a fading treasure.
    Siren pleasant, foe to reason,
    Cupid plague thee for thy treason.

Prime youth lasts not, age will follow,
And make white those tresses yellow;
Wrinkled face, for looks delightful,
Shall acquaint thee, dame despiteful!
And when time shall date thy glory,
Then, too late, thou wilt be sorry.
    Siren pleasant, foe to reason,
    Cupid plague thee for this treason.
THOMAS LODGE.

THE PASSIONATE SHEPHERD TO HIS LOVE.

COME live with me and be my love,
And we will all the pleasures prove,
That hills and valleys, dales and fields,
Woods or steepy mountains yields.

And we will sit upon the rocks,
Seeing the shepherds feed their flocks,
By shallow rivers, to whose falls
Melodious birds sing madrigals.

And I will make thee beds of roses,
And a thousand fragrant posies ;
A cap of flowers, and a kirtle
Embroidered all with leaves of myrtle.

A gown made of the finest wool,
Which from your pretty lambs we pull,
Fair linèd slippers for the cold,
With buckles of the purest gold.

A belt of straw and ivy buds,
With coral clasps, and amber studs ;
And if these pleasures may thee move,
Come live with me, and be my love.

The shepherds swains shall dance and sing
For thy delight each May morning ;
If these delights thy mind may move,
Come live with me and be my love.

KIT MARLOWE.

MENAPHORI'S SONG.

SOME say Love,
Foolish Love,
    Doth rule and govern all the gods ;
I say Love,
Inconstant Love,
    Sets men's senses far at odds ;

Some swear Love,
Smoothed-faced Love,
 Is sweetest sweet that man can have ;
I say Love,
Sour Love,
 Makes virtue yield as beauty's slave.
A bitter sweet, a folly worst of all,
That forceth wisdom to be folly's thrall.

Love is sweet !
Wherein sweet ?
 In fading pleasures that do pain ;
Beauty sweet !
Is that sweet
 That yieldeth sorrow for a gain ?
If love 's sweet,
Herein sweet,
 That minute's joys are monthly woes.
'Tis not sweet,
That is sweet,
 Now, where but repentance grows.
Then love who list, if beauty be so sour,
Labor for me, Love rest in prince's bower.

ROBERT GREENE.

4

THE SHEPHERD'S WIFE'S SONG.

FROM "THE MOURNING GARMENT."

AH, what is love? It is a pretty thing,
As sweet unto a shepherd as a king,
            And sweeter too;
For kings have cares that wait upon a crown,
And cares can make the sweetest love to frown;
            Ah then, ah then,
If country loves such sweet desires do gain,
What lady would not love a shepherd swain?

His flocks are folded; he comes home at night,
As merry as a king in his delight;
            And merrier too,
For kings bethink them what the state require,
Where shepherds careless carol by the fire.
            Ah then, ah then,
If country loves such sweet desires do gain,
What lady would not love a shepherd swain?

He kisseth first, then sits as blithe to eat
His cream and curds, as doth the king his meat;
            And blither too,
For kings have often fears when they do sup,
Where shepherds dread no poison in the cup;
            Ah then, ah then,
If country loves such sweet desires do gain,
What lady would not love a shepherd swain?

To bed he goes, as wanton then, I ween,
As is a king in dalliance with a queen;
      More wanton too,
For kings have many griefs affects to move,
Where shepherds have no greater grief than love.
      Ah then, ah then,
If country loves such sweet desires do gain,
What lady would not love a shepherd swain?

Upon his couch of straw he sleeps as sound
As doth the king upon his beds of down;
      More sounder too,
For cares cause kings full oft their sleep to spill,
Where weary shepherds lie and snort their fill.
      Ah then, ah then,
If country loves such sweet desires do gain,
What lady would not love a shepherd swain?

Thus with his wife, he spends the year as blithe
As doth the king at every tide or sith;
      And blither too,
For kings have wars and broils to take in hand,
When shepherds laugh and love upon the land;
      Ah then, ah then,
Since country loves such sweet desires do gain,
What lady would not love a shepherd swain?

ROBERT GREENE.

CUPID'S INGRATITUDE.

FROM "ORPHARION."

CUPID abroad was 'lated in the night,
　His wings were wet with ranging in the rain,
Harbor he sought, to 'me he took his flight
　To dry his plumes; I heard the boy complain;
I oped the door, and granted his desire;
I rose myself, and made the wag a fire.

Looking more narrow, by the fire's flame
　I spied his quiver hanging by his back;
Doubting the boy might my misfortune frame,
　I would have gone, for fear of farther wrack;
But what I dread did me, poor wretch, betide,
For forth he drew an arrow from his side.

He pierced the quick, and I began to start;
　A pleasing wound, but that it was too high;
His shaft procured a sharp, yet sugared smart;
　Away he flew; for why, his wings were dry;
But left the arrow sticking in my breast,
That sore I grieved I welcomed such a guest.
　　　　　　　　　　　ROBERT GREENE.

INFIDA'S SONG.

FROM " FRANCESCO'S FORTUNES."

SWEET Adon, darst not glance thine eye,
  N'osery vous, mon bel ami ?
Upon thy Venus that must die?
  Ie vows en prie, pity me ;
N'osery vous, mon bel, mon bel,
  N'osery vous, mon bel ami ?

See how sad thy Venus lies,
  N'osery vous, mon bel ami ?
Love in heart, and tears in eyes,
  Ie vous en prie, pity me ;
N'osery vous, mon bel, mon bel,
  N'osery vous mon bel ami ?

Thy face is fair, as Paphos' brooks,
  N'osery vous, mon bel ami ?
Wherein Fancy baits her hooks ;
  Ie vous en prie, pity me.
N'osery vous, mon bel, mon bel,
  N'osery vous, mon bel ami ?

Thy cheeks like cherries that do grow,
  N'osery vous, mon bel ami ?
Amongst the western mounts of snow,
  Ie vous en prie, pity me ;

N'osery vous, mon bel, mon bel,
　　N'osery vous, mon bel ami?

Thy lips vermilion, full of love,
　　N'osery vous, mon bel ami?
Thy neck as silver-white as dove;
　　Ie vous en prie, pity me;
N'osery vous, mon bel, mon bel,
　　N'osery vous, mon bel ami?

Thine eyes like flames of holy fires,
　　N'osery vous, mon bel ami?
Burn all my thoughts with sweet desires;
　　Ie vous en prie, pity me;
N'osery vous, mon bel, mon bel,
　　N'osery vous, mon bel ami?

All thy beauties sting my heart,
　　N'osery vous, mon bel ami?
I must die through Cupid's dart;
　　Ie vous en prie, pity me;
N'osery vous, mon bel, mon bel,
　　N'osery vous, mon bel ami?

Wilt thou let thy Venus die?
　　N'osery vous, mon bel ami?
Adon were unkind, say I,
　　Ie vous en prie, pity me;

N'osery vous, mon bel, mon bel,
N'osery vous, mon bel ami?

To let fair Venus die for woe,
    N'osery vous, mon bel ami?
That doth love sweet Adon so;
    Ie vous en prie, pity me;
N'osery vous, mon bel, mon bel,
    N'osery vous, mon bel ami?

                    ROBERT GREENE.

LOVE.

FROM "HYMEN'S TRIUMPH."

LOVE is a sickness full of woes,
    All remedies refusing;
A plant that with most cutting grows,
    Most barren with best using;
        Why so?
More we enjoy it, more it dies;
If not enjoyed it sighing cries,
        Hey, ho!

Love is a torment of the mind,
    A tempest everlasting;
And Jove has made it of a kind
    Not well, nor full, nor fasting;

    Why so?
More we enjoy it, more it dies;
If not enjoyed it sighing cries,
    Hey, ho!

SAMUEL DANIEL.

SONG.

FROM "LOVE'S LABOR LOST."

ON a day (alack the day!)
Love, whose month is ever May,
Spied a blossom, passing fair,
Playing in the wanton air;
Through the velvet leaves the wind,
All unseen, 'gan passage find,
That the lover, sick to death,
Wished himself the heaven's breath.
"Air," quoth he, "thy cheeks may blow;
Air, would I might triumph so!
But, alack, my hand is sworn,
Ne'er to pluck thee from thy thorn;
Vow, alack, for youth unmeet,
Youth, so apt to pluck a sweet.
Do not call it sin in me,
That I am forsworn for thee;
Thou, for whom Jove would swear
Juno but an Ethiop were,
And deny himself for Jove,
Turning mortal for thy love."

SHAKESPEARE.

THE KISS.

FROM "CYNTHIA'S REVELS."

O, THAT joy so soon should waste !
    Or so sweet a bliss
      As a kiss,
  Might not forever last.
So sugared, so melting, so soft, so delicious ;
  The dew that lies on roses,
  When the morn herself discloses
    Is not so precious.
  O, rather than I would it smother,
  Were I to taste such another,
    It should be my wishing
    That I might die with kissing.
BEN JONSON.

VENUS' RUNAWAY.

FROM " THE HUE AND CRY AFTER CUPID."

BEAUTIES, have you seen this toy,
Callèd Love, a little boy,
Almost naked, wanton, blind ;
Cruel now, and then as kind ?
If he be amongst ye, say,
He is Venus' runaway.

He hath marks about him plenty ;
You shall know him among twenty ;
All his body is a fire,
And his breath a flame entire,
That being shot, like lightning in,
Wounds the heart, but not the skin.

At his sight the sun hath turned,
Neptune, in the waters burned ;
Hell hath felt a greater heat ;
Jove himself forsook his seat ;
From the centre to the sky,
Are his trophies rearèd high.

Wings he hath, which though ye clip,
He will leap from lip to lip,
Over liver, lights, and heart,
But not stay in any part ;
And if chance his arrow misses,
He will shoot himself, in kisses.

He doth bear a golden bow,
And a quiver, hanging low,
Full of arrrows, that outbrave
Dian's shaft ; where, if he have
Any head more sharp than other,
With that first he strikes his mother.

Still the fairest are his fuel,
When his days are to be cruel;
Lover's hearts are all his food,
And his baths their warmest blood;
Naught but wounds his hand doth season,
And he hates none like to Reason.

Trust him not, his words, though sweet,
Seldom with his heart do meet;
All his practice is deceit,
Every gift it is a bait;
Not a kiss but poison bears,
And most treason in his tears.

Idle minutes are his reign;
Then, the straggler makes his gain
By presenting maids with toys,
And would have ye think them joys.
'Tis the ambition of the elf,
To have all childish as himself.

If by these ye please to know him,
Beauties, be not nice, but show him,
Though ye had a will to hide him,
Now, we hope, ye'll not abide him;
Since you hear his falser play,
And that he 's Venus' runaway.

BEN JONSON.

TO CELIA.

Drink to me only with thine eyes,
    And I will pledge with mine ;
Or leave a kiss but in the cup,
    And I'll not look for wine.
The thirst that from the soul doth rise,
    Doth ask a drink divine,
But might I of Jove's nectar sup,
    I would not change for thine.

I sent thee late a rosy wreath,
    Not so much honoring thee,
As giving it a hope, that there
    It could not withered be,
But thou thereon did'st only breathe,
    And sent'st it back to me ;
Since when, it grows and smells, I ween.
    Not of itself, but thee.

Ben Jonson.

TO ANGELINA.

FROM "THE ELDER BROTHER."

Beauty clear and fair,
    Where the air
Rather like a perfume dwells,
    Where the violet and the rose
    Their blue veins and blush disclose,
And come to honor nothing else.

Where to live near,
  And planted there,
Is still to live and still live new;
  Where to gain a favor is
  More than light, perpetual bliss,
O, make me live by serving you.

Dear, again back recall
  To this light.
A stranger to himself and all;
  Both the wonder and the story
  Shall be yours, and eke the glory;
I am your servant and your thrall.

BEAUMONT AND FLETCHER.

SPRING-TIME AND LOVE.

FROM "VALENTINIAN."

Now the lusty spring is seen,
  Golden yellow, gaudy blue,
  Daintily invite the view;
Everywhere, on every green,
Roses, blushing as they blow,
  And enticing men to pull;
Lilies, whiter than the snow,
  Woodbines, of sweet honey full;
All love's emblems, and all cry,
"Ladies, if not plucked, we die."

Yet the lusty spring has stayed ;
  Blushing red, and purest white,
  Daintily to love invite
Every woman, every maid.
Cherries, kissing as they grow,
  And inviting men to taste ;
Apples, even ripe below,
  Winding gently to the waist ;
All love's emblems, and all cry,
"Ladies, if not plucked, we die."

II.

Hear, ye ladies that despise,
  What the mighty Love has done ;
Fear examples, and be wise.
  Fair Caliston was a nun ;
Leda, sailing on a stream,
  To deceive the hopes of man,
Love accounting but a dream,
  Doted on a silver swan ;
Danae, in a brazen tower,
Where no love was, loved a flower.

Hear, ye ladies that are coy,
  What the mighty Love can do ;
Fear the fierceness of the boy,
  The chaste moon he makes to woo.

Vesta, kindling holy fires,
  Circled round about with spies,
Never dreaming loose desires,
  Doting, at the altar, dies.
Ilion in a short hour, higher
He can build, and once more fire.
                    BEAUMONT AND FLETCHER.

SONG.

O, DO not wanton with those eyes,
  Lest I be sick with seeing;
Nor cast them down, but let them rise,
  Lest shame destroy their being. •

O, be not angry with those fires,
  For then their threats will kill me,
Nor look too kind on my desires,
  For then my hopes will spill me.

O, do not steep them in thy tears,
  For so will sorrow slay me,
Nor spread them as distract with fears,
  Mine own enough betray me.
                    BEN JONSON.

TO A GLOVE.

FROM "CYNTHIA'S REVELS."

THOU more than most sweet glove
Unto my more sweet love,
Suffer me to store with kisses,
This empty lodging, that now misses
The pure rosy hand that wear thee,
Whiter than the kid that bear thee.
Thou art soft, but that was softer,
Cupid's self has kissed it ofter
Than e'er he did his mother's doves;
Supposing her the queen of loves,
That was thy mistress, best of gloves.

BEN JONSON.

THE "TRIUMPH OF CHARIS."

SEE the chariot at hand here of Love,
  Wherein my lady rideth!
Each that draws is a swan or a dove,
  And well the car Love guideth.
As she goes, all hearts do duty
      Unto her beauty,
And enamored do wish, so they might
      But enjoy such a sight,
That they still were to run by her side
Through swords, through seas, whither she would ride.

Do but look on her eyes, they do light
  All that Love's world compriseth!
Do but look on her hair, it is bright
  As Love's star, when it riseth!
Do but mark her forehead, smoother
      Than words that soothe her;
And from her arched brows, such a grace
      Sheds itself through the face,
As alone there triumphs to the life,
All the gain, all the good, of the elements' strife.

Have you seen but a bright lily grow,
  Before rude hands have touched it?
Have you marked but the fall of the snow,
  Before the soil hath smutched it?
Have you felt the wool of the beaver?
      Or swan's down ever?
Or have smelt o' the bud of the brier?
      Or the nard in the fire?
Or have tasted the bag of the bee?
O so white! O so soft! O so sweet is she!

                  BEN JONSON.

5

SONG.

FROM "THE BLOODY BROTHER."

TAKE, O, take those lips away,
   That so sweetly were forsworn,
And those eyes, like break of day,
   Lights that do mislead the morn ;
But my kisses bring again,
Seals of love, but sealed in vain.

Hide, O, hide those hills of snow,
   Which thy frozen bosom bears,
On whose tops the pinks that grow,
   Are yet of those that April wears ;
But first set my poor heart free,
Bound in those icy chains by thee.

BEAUMONT AND FLETCHER.

GREETINGS TO MY LOVE.

PACK clouds away, and welcome day,
   With night we banish sorrow ;
Sweet air blow soft, mount larks aloft,
   To give my love good-morrow !
Wings from the wind to please her mind,
   Notes from the lark, I'll borrow ; ·

Bird, prune thy wing, nightingale, sing,
   To give my love good-morrow!
   To give my love good-morrow,
Notes from them both I'll borrow.

Wake from thy nest, robin red-breast,
   Sing birds in every furrow,
And from each hill let music's thrill,
   Give my fair love good-morrow!
Blackbird and thrush, in every bush,
   Stare, linnet, and cock-sparrow,
Ye pretty elves, amongst yourselves,
   Sing my fair love good-morrow!
   To give my love good-morrow,
Sing birds in every furrow!

THOMAS HEYWOOD.

TO AURORA.

I SWEAR, Aurora, by thy starry eyes,
   And by those golden locks, whose lock none slips,
   And by the coral of thy rosy lips,
And by the naked snows which beauty dyes;

I swear by all the jewels of thy mind,
   Whose like yet never worldly treasure bought,
   Thy solid judgment, and thy generous thought,
Which in this darkened age have clearly shined;

I swear by those, and by my spotless love,
　And by my secret, yet most fervent fires,
　That I have never nursed but chaste desires,
And such as modesty might well approve :

Then since I love these virtuous parts in thee,
Shouldst thou not love this virtuous mind in me ?

WM. ALEXANDER, EARL OF STIRLING.

TO PHYLLIS.

FROM "THE FAIR MAID OF THE EXCHANGE."

YE little birds that sit and sing
　Amidst the shady valleys,
And see how sweetly Phyllis walks
　Within her garden alleys ;
Go, pretty birds, about her bower ;
Sing, pretty birds, she may not lower ;
Ah me ! methinks I see her frown ;
　Ye pretty wantons, warble.

Go tell her through your chirping bills,
　As you by me were bidden,
To her is only known my love,
　Which from the world is hidden.
Go, pretty birds, and tell her so,
See that your notes strain not too low,
For still methinks I see her frown ;
　Ye pretty wantons, warble.

Go, tune your voices' harmony,
    And sing I am her lover ;
Strain loud and sweet, that every note
    With sweet content may move her ;
And she that hath the sweetest voice,
Tell her I will not change my choice ;
Yet still methinks I see her frown ;
    Ye pretty wantons, warble.

O fly ! make haste ! see, see, she falls
    Into a pretty slumber,
Sing round about her rosy bed,
    That waking she may wonder ;
Say to her he 's her lover true,
That sendeth love to you, to you ;
And when you hear her kind reply,
    Return with pleasant warblings.

                    THOMAS HEYWOOD.

THE SIREN'S SONG.

FROM "A MASQUE OF THE INNER TEMPLE."

STEER, hither steer your wingèd pines,
    All beaten mariners !
Here lie Love's undiscovered mines,
    A prey to passengers ;
Perfumes far sweeter than the best,
Which make the Phœnix' urn and nest ;

Fear not your ships,
Nor any to oppose you, save our lips,
But come on shore,
Where no joy dies till love hath gotten more ;
For swelling waves, our panting breasts,
Where never storms arise,
Exchange, and be awhile our guests ;
For stars, gaze on our eyes ;
The compass, Love shall hourly sing,
And as he goes about the ring,
We will not miss
To tell each point he nameth, with a kiss.
Then come on shore,
Where no joy dies till love has gotten more.

WILLIAM BROWNE.

SONG.

FROM "THE OLD COUPLE."

DEAR, do not your fair beauty wrong
In thinking you are still too young!
The rose and lilies in your cheek
Flourish, and no more ripeness seek.

Your cherry lip, red, soft, and sweet,
Proclaims such fruit for taste most meet ;
Then lose no time, for Love has wings,
And flies away from aged things.

THOMAS MAY.

VENUS' RUNAWAYS.

FROM "CUPID AND PSYCHE."

I.

CUPID.

THE wanton Cupid, t'other day,
Did from his mother Venus stray ;
Great pains she took, but all in vain,
How to get her son again ;
For since the boy is sometimes blind,
He his own way cannot find.
If any one can fetch him in,
Or take him captive in a gin,
And bring her word, she for this
Will reward him with a kiss.

That you the felon may descry,
These are the signs to know him by :
His skin is red with many a stain
Of lovers, which by him were slain,
Or else it is the fatal doom,
Which foretells of storms to come ;
Though he seem naked to the eye,
His mind is clothed in subtlety ;
Sweet speech he useth and soft smiles,
To entice where he beguiles ;
His words are gentle as the air,
But trust him not, though he speak fair,

And confirm it with an oath.
He is fierce and cruel both ;
He is bold and careless too,
And will play as wantons do ;
But when you think the sport is past,
It turns to earnest at the last.

His evil nature none can tame,
For neither reverence or shame
Are in his looks ; his curlèd hair
Hangs like nets for to ensnare ;
His hands, though weak and slender, strike
Ages and sexes, all alike ;
And when he list, he'll make his nest
In their marrow, or their breast ;
Those poisoned darts shot from his bow,
Hurt gods above, and men below.

His left hand bears a flaming torch,
Whose flame the very same will scorch,
And not hell itself is free
From this imp's impiety.
The wounds he makes, no salve can cure.
Then if you catch him, bind him sure ;
Take no pity though he cry,
Or laugh, or smile, or seem to die,
And for his ransom would deliver,
His arrows and his painted quiver ;

Refuse them all, for they are such
That will burn whate'er they touch.

II.

PSYCHE.

O yes! if any can true tidings bring
Of Venus' handmaid, daughter to a king, —
Psyche, the fugitive, of stature tall,
Of tender age, and form celestial ;
To whom for dowry, Art and Nature gave
All grace, and all the comeliness they have ;
This I was bid to say, and be it spoken
Without all envy, each smile is a token
Sufficient to betray her. In her gait
She Phœbus' sister doth most imitate.

Nor does her voice sound mortal ; if you spy
Her face you may discern her by the eye,
That, like a star, dazzles the optic sense, —
Cupid has oft his torch brought lighted thence.
If any find her out, let him repair
Straightways to Mercury, and the news declare ;
And for his recompense, he shall have leave
Even from Venus' own lips to receive
Seven fragrant kisses, and the rest among
One honey kiss, and one touch from her tongue.

SHAKERLEY MARMION.

SONG.

FROM " AGLAURA."

WHY so pale and wan, fond lover?
  Prythee, why so pale?
Will, when looking well can't move her,
  Looking ill prevail?
  Prythee why so pale?

Why so dull and mute, young sinner?
  Prythee, why so mute?
Will, when speaking well can't move her,
  Saying nothing do't?

Quit, quit, for shame! this will not move,
  This cannot take her.
If of herself she will not love,
  Nothing can make her.
  The devil take her.

                    SIR JOHN SUCKLING.

SEND BACK MY HEART. — SONG.

I PRYTHEE send me back my heart,
  Since I cannot have thine,
For if from yours you will not part,
  Why then shouldst thou have mine?

Yet now I think on't, let it lie,
  To find it were in vain,
For thou'st a thief in either eye
  Would steal it back again.

Why should two hearts in one breast lie,
  And yet not lodge together?
O Love, where is thy sympathy,
  If thus our breasts thou sever?

But love is such a mystery
  I cannot find it out,
For when I think I'm best resolved
  I then am most in doubt.

Then farewell care, and farewell woe,
  I will no longer pine ;
For I'll believe I have her heart,
  As much as she has mine.

               ·SIR JOHN SUCKLING.

THE INDIFFERENT.

TELL me not of a face that's fair,
  Nor lip and cheek that's red,
Nor of the tresses of her hair,
  Nor curls in order laid ;

Nor of a rare seraphic voice,
   That like an angel sings,
Though if I were to take my choice,
   I would have all these things;
But if that thou wilt have me love,
   And it must be a she,
The only argument can move,
   Is, that she will love me.

The glories of your ladies be
   But metaphors of things,
And but resemble what we see
   Each common object brings.
Roses out-red their lips and cheeks,
   Lilies their whiteness stain,
What fool is he that shadows seeks,
   And may the substance gain.
Then if thou'lt have me love a lass, .
   Let it be one that's kind,
Else I'm a servant to the glass,
   That's with Canary lined.

                  ALEXANDER BROWNE.

THE DYING LOVER.

DEAR love, let me this evening die!
   O smile not to prevent it;
Dead with my rivals let me lie,
   Or we shall both repent it.

Frown quickly then, and break my heart,
   That so my way of dying
May, though my life was full of smart,
   Be worth the world's enoying.

And now let lovers ring their bells,
   For me, poor youth, departed,
Who kindly in his love excels,
   By dying broken-hearted.
My grave with flowers, let virgins strew,
   Which, if thy tears fall near them,
May so transcend in scent and show,
   As thou wilt shortly wear them.

Such flowers, how much will florists prize,
   Which on a lover growing,
Are watered with his mistress' eyes,
   With pity ever flowing.
A grave, so decked, will, though thou art
   Yet fearful to come nigh me,
Provoke thee straight to break thy heart,
   And lie down boldly by me.

Then everywhere all bells shall ring,
   All light to darkness turning,
Whilst every choir shall sadly sing,
   And Nature's self wear mourning.

Yet we hereafter may be found
  By destiny's right placing,
Making, like flowers, love under ground,
  Whose roots are still embracing.

SIR WILLIAM DAVENANT.

THE MAID'S RESOLUTION.

FROM "THE UNFORTUNATE LOVERS."

'TIS in good truth a most wonderful thing
  (I am e'en ashamed to relate it),
That Love so many vexations should bring,
  And yet few have the wit to hate it.

Love's weather, in maids should seldom hold fair,
  Like April's mine quickly shall alter,
I'll give him to-night a lock of my hair,
  To whom, next day, I'll send a halter.

I cannot abide these malapert males,
  Pirates of love, who know no duty,
Till love, with a storm, can take down their sails,
  And they must strike to Admiral Beauty.

Farewell to that maid who will be undone,
  Who, in markets of men (where plenty
Are cried up and down) will die even for one, —
  I will live to make fools of twenty.

SIR WILLIAM DAVENANT.

LOVE'S SIGNS.

FROM "THE LADY-ERRANT."

To carve our loves in myrtle rinds,
   And tell our secrets to the woods ;
To send our sighs by faithful winds,
   And trust our tears unto the floods ;
     To call where no man hears,
     And think the rocks have ears ;
To walk, and rest, to live and die,
And yet not know whence, how, or why ;
To have our hopes with fears still checked,
To credit doubts, and truth suspect, —
     This, this, is what we may
     A lover's absence say.
  Follies without are cares within,
  Where eyes do fail, there souls begin.

WILLIAM CARTWRIGHT.

THE SWEET NEGLECT.

FROM "THE SILENT WOMAN."

STILL to be neat, still to be drest
As you were going to a feast ;
Still to be powdered, still perfumed,
Lady, it is to be presumed,
Though art's hid causes are not found,
All is not sweet, all is not sound.

Give me a look, give me a face,
That makes simplicity a grace ;
Robes loosely flowing, hair as free ;
Such sweet neglect more taketh me
Than all the adulteries of art.
They strike mine eyes, but not my heart.

BEN JONSON.

THE REWARD OF INNOCENT LOVE.

FROM "CASTARA."

WE saw and wooed each other's eyes,
  My soul contracted then with thine,
And both burnt in one sacrifice,
  By which the marriage grew divine.

Time 's ever ours while we despise
  The sensual idol of our clay ;
For though our sun doth set and rise,
  We joy an everlasting day,

Whose light no jealous clouds obscure ;
  While each of us shine innocent,
The troubled stream is still impure ;
  With virtue flies away content.

And though opinion often err,
  We'll court the modest smile of fame ;

For sin's black danger circles her
  Who hath infection in her name.

Thus when to one dark, silent room,
  Death shall our loving coffins thrust,
Fame will build columns on our tomb,
  And add a perfume to our dust.

WILLIAM HABINGTON.

TO ROSES IN CASTARA'S BOSOM.

YE blushing virgins happy are
  In the chaste nunnery of her breast,
For he'd profane so chaste a fair
  Who e'er should call them Cupid's nest.

Transplanted thus, how bright ye grow,
  How rich a fragrance do ye yield,
In some close garden. cowslips so
  Are sweeter than i' the open field.

In those white cloisters live secure
  From the rude blasts of wanton. breath,
Each hour more innocent and pure,
  Till you shall wither into death.

6

Then that which living gave you room
   Your glorious sepulchre should be ;
There wants no marble for a tomb
   Whose breast hath marble been to me.
WILLIAM HABINGTON.

CRUSHED FLOWERS.

THOSE whiter lilies, which the early morn
   Seems to have newly woven of cleaved silk,
To which on banks of wealthy Tagus born,
   Gold was their cradle, liquid pearl their milk ;
The blushing roses, with whose virgin leaves
   The wanton Wind to sport himself presumes,
Whilst from their rifled wardrobe he receives,
   For his wings, purple, for his breath, perfumes,—

Both those and these, my Celia's pretty foot
   Trod up : but if she should again her face display,
And fragrant breast, they'd die again to the root,
   As with the blasting of the mid-day's ray ;
And the soft wind which both perfumes and cools,
Pass like the unregarded breath of fools.
SIR RICHARD FANSHAWE.

THE FAIR SHEPHERDESS.

FROM " THEODOSIUS."

HAIL to the myrtle shades !
All hail to the nymphs of the fields !
Kings would not here invade
Those pleasures that virtue yields.

Beauty here opens her arms,
To soften the languishing mind,
And Phillis unlocks her charms, —
Ah Phillis ! ah why so kind ?

Phillis, thou soul of love,
Thou joy of the neighboring swains ;
Phillis, that crowns the grove,
And Phillis that gilds the plains.

Phillis, that ne'er had the skill
To paint, to patch, and be fine,
Yet Phillis whose eyes can kill,
Whom nature hath made divine.

Phillis, whose charming song
Makes labor and pain a delight ;
Phillis that makes the day young,
And shortens the livelong night.

Phillis, whose lips, like May,
  Still laugh at the sweets that they bring ;
Where love never knows decay,
  But sets with eternal spring.

NATHANIEL LEE.

THE MAID'S WARNING.

FROM "THE MAN OF MODE."

As Amores with Phyllis sat,
  One evening on the plain,
And saw the charming Strephon wait
  To tell the nymph his pain,

The threatened danger to remove
  She whispered in her ear,
"Ah, Phyllis, if you would not have
  This shepherd, do not hear.

"None ever had so strange an art
  His passion to convey
Into a listening virgin's heart
  And steal her soul away.

"Fly, fly betimes, for fear you give
  Occasion for your fate."
"In vain," said she, "in vain I strive ;
  Alas ! 'tis *now* too late."

SIR CHARLES SEDLEY.

SONG.

LOVE still hath something of the sea
   From which his mother rose,
No time his slaves from doubt can free,
   Nor give their thoughts repose.

They are becalmed in clearest days,
   And in rough weather tossed;
They wither under cold delays,
   Or are in tempests lost.

One while they seem to touch the port;
   Then straight into the main,
Some angry wind, in cruel sport,
   The vessel drives again.

At first Disdain and Pride they fear,
   Which if they chance to 'scape,
Rivals and Falsehood soon appear,
   In a more cruel shape.

By such degrees to joy they come,
   And are so long withstood,
So slowly they receive the sum,
   It hardly does them good.

'Tis cruel to prolong a pain:
   And to defer a joy,

Believe me, gentle Celemene,
Offends the wingèd boy.

A hundred thousand oaths your fears
Perhaps would not remove ;
And if I gazed a thousand years,
I could not deeper love.

SIR CHARLES SEDLEY.

CLARINDA.

FROM " KING ARTHUR."

O SIGHT, the mother of desires,
What charming objects dost thou yield !
'Tis sweet, when tedious night expires,
To see the rosy morning gild
The mountains tops, and paint the fields.
But when Clarinda comes in sight,
She makes the summer's day more bright,
And when she goes away, 'tis night.

'Tis sweet the blushing morn to view,
And plains adorned with pearly dew ;
But such cheap delights to see,
Heaven and nature
Give each creature ;
They have eyes as well as we.

This is the joy, all joys above,
    To seè, to see,
      That only she,
   That only she we love!

JOHN DRYDEN.

JEALOUSY.

FROM "LOVE TRIUMPHANT."

WHAT state of life can be so blest
As love, that warms the lover's breast?
Two souls in one, the same desire
To grant the bliss and to require!
But if in heaven a hell we find,
'Tis all from thee,
O Jealousy!
'Tis all from thee,
O Jealousy!
Thou tyrant, tyrant Jealousy,
Thou tyrant of the mind!

All other ills, though sharp they prove;
Serve to refine, and perfect love;
In absence, or unkind disdain,
Sweet hope relieves the lover's pain;
But, ah! no cure but death we find,
To set us free
From Jealousy;

O Jealousy!
Thou tyrant, tyrant Jealousy,
Thou tyrant of the mind!

False in thy glass all objects are,
Some set too near, and some too far ;
Thou art the fire of endless night,
The fire that burns, and gives no light ;
All torments of the damned we find
In only thee,
O Jealousy!
Thou tyrant, tyrant Jealousy,
Thou tyrant of the mind.

JOHN DRYDEN.

THE THIEF.

THOU robb'st my days of business and delights ;
Of sleep thou robb'st my nights.
Ah, lovely thief, what wilt thou do ?
What, rob me of Heaven ! too ?
Thou even my prayers dost steal from me,
And I, with wild idolatry,
Begin to God, and end them all to thee.

Is it a sin to love, that it should thus
Like an ill conscience torture us ?
Whate'er I do, where'er I go
(None guiltless e'er was haunted so),

Still, still, methinks thy face I view,
And still thy shape doth me pursue,
As if, not you me, but *I* had murdered you.

From books I strive some remedy to take,
But thy name all the letters make
Whate'er is writ ; I find *that* there,
Like points and commas, everywhere.
Me blest for this, let no man hold,
For I, as Midas did of old,
Perish by turning everything to gold.

A. COWLEY.

INCONSTANCY.

FROM " MUCH ADO ABOUT NOTHING."

SIGH no more, ladies, sigh no more, —
    Men were deceivers ever ;
One foot in sea, and one on shore,
    To one thing constant never :
        Then sigh not so,
        But let them go,
    And be you blithe and bonny,
Converting all your sounds of woe
    Into hey nonny, nonny !

Sing no more ditties, sing no mo'
    Of dumps, so dull and heavy ;

The fraud of men was ever so,
　　Since summer first was leavy :
　　　Then sigh not so,
　　　But let them go,
　　And be you blithe and bonny,
Converting all your sounds of woe
　　Into hey nonny, nonny!

SHAKESPEARE.

COME, NIGHT.

FROM "HERO AND LEANDER."

COME, come, dear Night! Love's mart of kisses,
　　Sweet close of his ambitious line ;
The beautiful summer of his blisses
　　Love's glory does in darkness shine.
O come, soft rest of cares! come, Night!
　　Come, naked virtue's only tire,
The reapèd harvest of the light,
　　Bound up in sheaves of sacred fire.
　　　　Love calls to war,
　　　　　Sighs, his alarms,
　　　　　Lips, his swords are,
　　　　　　The field, his arms.

Come, Night, and lay thy velvet hand
　　On glorious Day's out-facing face ;
And all thy crownèd flames command
　　For torches to our nuptial grace.

Love calls to war,
　　Sighs, his alarms,
Lips, his swords are,
　　The field, his arms.

No need have we of factious Day,
　To cast, in envy of thy peace,
Her balls of discord in thy way ;
　Her beauty's day doth never cease.
　　Love calls to war,
　　　Sighs, his alarms,
　　Lips, his swords are,
　　　The field, his arms.

　　The evening star I see ;
　　　Rise, youths ! the evening star
　　Helps Love to summon War,
　　　Both now embracing be.

Rise, youths ! Love's rites claim more than ban-
　　　quets ; rise !
Now the bright marigolds that deck the skies,
Phœbus' celestial flowers, that (contrary
To his flowers here) ope when he shuts his eye,
And shuts when he does open, crown your sports ;
Now Love in Night, and Night in Love, exhorts.
Courtship and dances all your powers employ,
And suit Night's rich expansure with your joy ;

Love paints his longings in sweet virgin's eyes ;
Rise, youths ! Love's rites claim more than ban-
    quets ; rise !

GEORGE CHAPMAN.

SONG OF JUNO AND CERES.

FROM " THE TEMPEST."

JUNO.

HONOR, riches, marriage-blessing,
Long continuance, and increasing,
Hourly joys be still upon you !
Juno sings her blessings on you.

CERES.

Earth's increase, foison plenty,
Barns and garners never empty ;
Vines, with clust'ring bunches growing ;
Plants, with goodly burthen bowing :
Spring come to you, at the farthest,
In the very end of harvest !
Scarcity and want shall shun you ;
Ceres' blessing so is on you.

SHAKESPEARE.

SONG.

FROM "THE TWO NOBLE KINSMEN."

ROSES, their sharp spines being gone,
Not royal in their smells alone,
            But in their hue ;
Maiden pinks, of odor faint,
Daisies smelless, but most quaint,
            And sweet thyme true ;

Primrose, first-born child of Ver,
Merry spring-time's harbinger,
            With her bells dim ;
Oxlips, in their cradle growing,
Marigolds, on death-beds blowing,
            Lark heels trim, —

All dear Nature's children sweet,
Lie 'fore bride and bridegroom's feet,
            Blessing their sense.
Not an angel of the air,
Bird melodious, or bird fair,
            Be absent hence.

The crow, nor slanderous cuckoo, nor
The boding raven, nor chough hoar,
            Nor chattering pie

May on our bird-house perch or sing,
Or with them any discord bring,
    But from it fly.
              BEAUMONT AND FLETCHER.

HYMEN'S BLESSING.

FROM "THE BROKEN HEART."

COMFORTS lasting, loves increasing,
Like soft hours, never ceasing ;
Plenty's pleasure, peace complying
Without jars, or tongues envying :
Hearts by holy union wedded,
More than theirs by custom bedded ;
Fruitful issues, life so graced,
Not by time to be defaced ;
Budding as the year ensu'th
Every spring, another youth, —
All what thought can add beside,
Crown this bridegroom and this bride.
              JOHN FORD.

Songs of
Feeling
&
Thought

SONGS

OF

THOUGHT AND FEELING.

———————

THE ANGER OF FRIENDS IS THE RENEWING OF LOVE.

IN "PARADISE OF DAINTY DEVICES."

IN going to my naked bed as one that would have
    slept,
I heard a wife sing to her child that long before had
    wept,
She sighèd sore, and sang full sweet, to bring the babe
    to rest,
That would not rest, but crièd still, in sucking at her
    breast:
She was full weary with her watch, and grievèd with
    her child,
She rockèd it; and rated it until on her it smiled;
Then did she say, "Now have I found the proverb
    true to prove,
'The falling out of faithful friends, renewing is of
    love.'"

Then took I paper, pen, and ink, this proverb for to
    write,
In register for to remain of such a worthy night ;
As she proceeded thus in song unto her little brat,
Much matter uttered she of weight, in place whereas
    she sat ;
And provèd plain, there was no beast, nor creature
    bearing life
Could well be known to live in love, without discord
    or strife ;
Then kissed she her little babe, and swore by God
    above,
" The falling out of faithful friends, renewing is of
    Love."

RICHARD EDWARDS.

LULLABY OF A LOVER.

SING lullaby, as women do
    Wherewith they bring their babes to rest ;
And lullaby can I sing too,
    As womanly as can the best.
With lullaby they still the child ;
And if I be not much beguiled,
Full many wanton babes have I
Which must be stilled with lullaby.

First, lullaby my youthful years,
  It is now time to go to bed ;
For crooked age and hoary hairs
  Have now the haven within my head ;
With lullaby then youth be. still,
With lullaby content thy will
Since courage quails, and comes behind ;
Go sleep, and so beguile thy mind.

Next, lullaby my gazing eyes,
  Which wonted were to glance apace,
For every glass may now suffice
  To show the furrows in my face.
With lullaby then wink a while,
With lullaby your looks beguile, .
Let no fair face, nor beauty bright,
Entice you eft with vain delight.

And lullaby my wanton will,
  Let reason's rule now reign my thought
Since all too late I find by skill
  How dear I have thy fancies bought ;
With lullaby, now take thine ease,
With lullaby, thy doubts appease,
For trust to this, if thou be still
My body shall obey thy will.

GEORGE GASCOIGNE.

7

ADIEU TO CARE.

CARE, care, go pack! thou art no mate for me,
  Thy thorny thoughts the heart to death do wound;
Thou mak'st the fair seem like a blasted tree,
  By thee green years with hoary hairs are crowned;
    Which makes me sing, to solace mine annoy,
    Care, care, adieu! — my heart doth hope for joy.

Care, care, adieu! thou rival of delight!
  Return into the cave of deep despair;
Thou art no guest to harbor near my spright,
  Whose poison sighs infect the very air:
    Wherefore I sing, to solace mine annoy,
    Care, care, adieu! — my heart doth hope for joy.

Care, care, adieu! and welcome pleasure now,
  Thou wish of joy and ease of pleasure both,
To wear thy weed I make a solemn vow,
  Let time or chance be pleasèd or be wroth:
    And therefore sing, to solace mine annoy,
    Care, care, adieu! — my heart doth hope for joy.

                    GEORGE WHETSTONE.

SPRING AND MELANCHOLY.

THE earth, late choked with showers,
  Is now arrayed in green ;
Her bosom springs with flowers,
  The air dissolves her teen,
    The heavens laugh at her glory ;
    Yet bide I sad and sorry.

The woods are decked with leaves,
  The trees are clothèd gay ;
And Flora crowned with sheaves
  With oaken boughs doth play ;
    Where I am clad in black
    In token of my wrack.

The birds upon the trees,
  Do sing with pleasant voices,
And chant in their degrees,
  Their loves and lucky choices
    When I, whilst they are singing,
    With sighs mine arms am wringing.

The thrushes seek the shade,
  And I my fatal grave ;
Their flight to heaven is made,
  My walk on earth I have,

They free ; I thrall ; they jolly ;
I sad and pensive wholly.

THOMAS LODGE.

THE AGED COURTIER.

FROM A PAGEANT IN HONOR OF QUEEN ELIZABETH.

His golden locks time hath to silver turned ;
  O time too swift ! O swiftness never ceasing !
His youth 'gainst time and aye hath ever spurned,
  But spurned in vain, youth waneth by increasing.
Beauty, strength, youth, are flowers but fading seen,
Duty, faith, love, are roots, and ever green.

His helmet now shall make a hive for bees ;
  And lovers' sonnets turned to holy psalms,
A man at arms, must now serve on his knees,
  And feed on prayers, which are aye his alms ;
But though from court to cottage he depart,
His saint is sure of his unspotted heart.

And when he saddest sits in holy cell,
  He'll teach his swains this carol for a song ;
Blest be the hearts that wish my sovereign well,
  Cursed be the souls that think her any wrong,
Goddess allow this aged man his right,
To be your beads-man now, that was your knight.

GEORGE PEELE.

THE PENITENT PALMER.

FROM "FRANCESCO'S FORTUNES."

WHILOM in the winter's rage
A Palmer, old and full of age,
Sat and thought upon his youth,
With eyes' tears, and heart's ruth,
Being all with cares y-blent,
When he thought on years misspent,
When his follies came to mind,
How fond love had made him blind,
And wrapped him in a field of woes
Shadowed with pleasure's shows.
Then he sighed, and said, " Alas !
Man is sin, and flesh is grass.
I thought my mistress' hairs were gold,
And in the locks my heart I fold ;
Her amber tresses were the sight
That wrappèd me in vain delight ;
Her ivory front, her pretty chin,
Were stales that drew me on to sin.
Her face was fair, her breath was sweet,
All her looks for love were meet,
But love is folly, this I know,
And beauty fadeth like to snow ;
O, why should man delight in pride,
Whose blossom like a dew doth glide ?

When these supposes touched my thought,
That world was vain, and beauty nought,
I 'gan sigh, and say, alas!
"Man is sin and flesh is grass."

ROBERT GREENE.

BEAUTY.

FROM "THE PASSIONATE PILGRIM."

BEAUTY is but a vain and doubtful good,
A shining gloss, that vadeth suddenly;
A flower that dies, when first it 'gins to bud;
A brittle glass that's broken presently;
    A doubtful good, a gloss, a glass, a flower,
    Lost, vaded, broken, dead, within an hour,

And as goods lost, are seld or never found,
As vaded gloss no rubbing will refresh,
As flowers dead, lie withered on the ground,
As broken glass no cement can redress,
    So beauty blemished once, forever's lost,
    In spite of physic, painting, pain, and cost.

SHAKESPEARE.

TO MUSIC.

FROM "HENRY VIII."

ORPHEUS with his lute made trees,
And the mountain-tops that freeze,
    Bow themselves when he did sing ;
To his music plants and flowers
Ever sprung ; as sun and showers
    There had made a lasting spring.

Everything that heard him play,
Even the billows of the sea,
    Hung their heads, and then lay by.
In sweet music is such art,
Killing care and grief of heart
    Fall asleep, or, hearing, die.

SHAKESPEARE.

SONGS OF AMIENS.

FROM "AS YOU LIKE IT."

I.

THE FOREST.

UNDER the greenwood tree,
    Who loves to lie with me,
And turn his merry note
    Unto the sweet bird's throat,

Come hither, come hither, come hither!
Here shall he see
No enemy,
But winter and rough weather.

Who doth ambition shun,
And loves to live i' the sun,
Seeking the food he eats,
And pleased with what he gets,
Come hither, come hither, come hither!
Here shall he see
No enemy,
But winter and rough weather.

II.

INGRATITUDE.

BLOW, blow, thou winter wind,
Thou art not so unkind
As man's ingratitude ;
Thy tooth is not so keen,
Because thou art not seen,
Although thy breath is rude.
Heigh-ho! sing heigh-ho! unto the green holly:
Most friendship is feigning, most loving mere folly ;
Then heigh-ho! the holly!
This life is most jolly.

Freeze, freeze, thou bitter sky,
Thou dost not bite so nigh,
　　As benefits forgot ;
Though thou the waters warp,
Thy sting is not so sharp
　　As friend remembered not.
Heigh-ho ! sing heigh-ho ! unto the green holly,
Most friendship is feigning, most loving mere folly ;
　　Then heigh-ho ! the holly !
　　This life is most jolly.

SHAKESPEARE.

FANCY.

FROM "MERCHANT OF VENICE."

TELL me where is Fancy bred,
In the heart, or in the head ?
How begot, how nourished ? —
　　Reply, reply.

It is engendered in the eyes ;
With gazing fed ; and Fancy dies
In the cradle where it lies.
Let us all ring Fancy's knell,
I'll begin it — Ding, dong, bell,
　　Ding, dong, bell,

SHAKESPEARE.

THE NIGHTINGALE AND THE POET.

As it fell upon a day,
In the merry month of May,
Sitting in a pleasant shade,
Which a grove of myrtles made,
Beasts did leap, and birds did sing,
Trees did grow, and plants did spring ;
Everything did banish moan,
Save the nightingale alone ;
She, poor bird, all, all forlorn,
Leaned her breast up till a thorn ;
And there sung the dolefull'st ditty,
That to hear it was great pity :
" Fie, fie, fie," now would she cry,
" Teru, teru !" by and by :
That to hear her so complain,
Scarce I could from tears refrain ;
For her griefs so lively shown,
Made me think upon mine own.
Ah ! thought I, thou mourn'st in vain ;
None take pity on thy pain ;
Senseless trees, they cannot hear thee ;
Ruthless bears, they will not cheer thee :
King Pandion, he is dead ;
All thy friends are lapped in lead ;
All thy fellow-birds do sing,

Careless of thy sorrowing.
Even so, poor bird, like thee,
None alive will pity me.
Whilst as fickle fortune smiled,
Thou and I were both beguiled.
Every one that flatters thee,
Is no friend in misery.
Words are easy as the wind,
Faithful friends are hard to find.
Every man will be thy friend,
While thou hast wherewith to spend ;
But if store of crowns be scant,
No man will supply thy want.
If that one be prodigal,
Bountiful they will him call ;
And with such like flattering,
" Pity but he were a king."
If he be addict to vice,
Quickly him they will entice ;
If to woman he be bent,
They have [him] at commandment.
But if fortune once do frown,
Then farewell his great renown :
They that frowned on him before,
Use his company no more.
He that is thy friend indeed,
He will help thee in thy need ;
If thou sorrow, he will weep :

If thou wake, he cannot sleep ;
Thus of every grief, in heart
He, with thee, doth bear a part, —
These are certain signs to know
Faithful friend from flattering foe.

RICHARD BARNFIELD.

CHORUS.

FROM "MIRIAM, THE FAIR MAID OF JEWRY."

THE fairest action of our human life,
   Is scorning to revenge an injury ;
For who forgives without a further strife,
   His adversary's heart doth to him tie :
And 'tis a firmer conquest, truly said,
To win the heart than overthrow the head.

If we a worthy enemy do find
   To yield to worth, it must be nobly done ;
But if of baser metal be his mind,
   In base revenge there is no honor won.
Who would a worthy courage overthrow,
And who would wrestle with a worthless foe ?

We say our hearts are great, and cannot yield.
   Because they cannot yield, it proves them poor :
Great hearts are lashed beyond their power but seld;
   The weakest lion will the loudest roar.

Truth's school for certain doth this same allow,
Highheartedness doth sometime teach to bow.

A noble heart doth teach a virtuous scorn :
  To scorn to owe a duty over long ;
To scorn to be for benefits forborne ;
  To scorn to lie ; to scorn to do a wrong ;
To scorn to bear an injury in mind ;
To scorn a free-born heart, slave-like to bind.

But if for wrongs we needs redress must have,
  Then be our vengeance of the noblest kind ;
Do we his body from our vengeance save,
  And let our hate prevail against his mind.
What can 'gainst him a greater vengeance be,
Than make his foe more worthy far than he ?

Lady Elizabeth Carew.

ADIEU TO LOVE.

FROM "THE LOVER'S PROGRESS."

Adieu, fond love ! farewell, you wanton power !
        I am free again,
Thou dull disease of blood and idle hours,
        Bewitching pain.
Fly to the fools that sigh away their time,
My nobler love to heaven climb
    And there behold beauty still young

That time can ne'er corrupt nor death destroy;
  Immortal sweetness by fair angels sung,
And honored by eternity and joy!
There lives my love, thither my hopes aspire,
Fond love declines, this heavenly love grows higher.
BEAUMONT AND FLETCHER.

TO SLEEP.

FROM " VALENTINIAN."

CARE-CHARMING sleep, thou easer of all woes,
Brother to Death, sweetly thyself dispose
On this afflicted Prince; fall like a cloud
In gentle showers; give nothing that is loud
Or painful to his slumbers; easy, sweet,
And as purling stream, thou son of Night
Pass by his troubled senses, sing his pain
Like hollow murmuring wind, or silver rain;
Into this prince gently, O, gently glide,
And kiss him into slumbers like a bride.
BEAUMONT AND FLETCHER.

WEEP NO MORE.

FROM "THE QUEEN OF CORINTH."

WEEP no more, nor sigh, nor groan,
Sorrow recalls no time that's gone;
Violet's plucked, the sweetest rain,
Makes not fresh nor grow again;

Trim thy locks, look cheerfully,
Fate's hidden ends eyes cannot see.
Joy as wingèd dreams fly fast,
Why should sadness longer last?
Grief is but a mound to woe;
Gentlest fair, mourn, mourn no more.

BEAUMONT AND FLETCHER.

ODE TO MELANCHOLY.

FROM "THE NICE VALOUR."

HENCE, all you vain delights,
As short as are the nights
    Wherein you spend your folly!
There 's nought in this life sweet,
If men were wise to see't,
    But only melancholy;
    O sweetest melancholy!

Welcome folded arms, and fixèd eyes,
A sigh that piercing mortifies,
A look that 's fastened to the ground,
A tongue chained up without a sound!
Fountain-heads, and pathless groves,
Places that pale passion loves!
Moonlight walks, where all the fowls
Are warmly housed, save bats and owls!

A midnight bell, a parting groan!
These are the sounds we feed upon;
Then stretch our bones in a still gloomy valley,
Nothing 's so dainty sweet as lovely melancholy.

BEAUMONT AND FLETCHER.

ANSWER TO ODE TO MELANCHOLY.

RETURN, my joys! and hither bring,
A tongue not made to speak, but sing,
A jolly spleen, an inward feast,
A careless laugh without a jest,
A face which gladness doth anoint,
An arm for joy flung out of joint,
A sprightful gait, that leaves no print,
And makes a feather of a flint;
A heart that 's lighter than the air,
An eye still dancing in its sphere,
Strong mirth, which nothing can control,
A body nimbler than a soul;
Free wandering thoughts not tied to muse, ·
Which, thinking all things, nothing choose,
Which, ere we see them come, are gone;—
These, life itself doth feed upon,
Then take no care but only to be jolly;
To be more wretched than we must, is folly.

WILLIAM STRODE.

COME, SLEEP.

FROM " THE WOMAN HATER."

COME, sleep, and with thy sweet deceiving
    Lock me in delight a while ;
    Let some pleasing dreams beguile
    All my fancies, that from thence,
    I may feel an influence,
All my powers of care bereaving.

Though but a shadow, but a sliding,
    Let me know some little joy ;
    We that suffer long annoy,
    Are contented with a thought
    Through an idle fancy wrought ;
O, let my joys have some abiding.

              BEAUMONT AND FLETCHER.

TO MUSIC.

WHEN whispering strains do softly steal
    With creeping passion through the heart,
And when at every touch we feel
    Our pulses beat, and bear a part ;
        When threads can make
        A heart-string quake,
        Philosophy
        Can scarce deny,
Our souls consist of harmony.

8

O lull, lull, lull me, charming air,
  My senses rock with wonder sweet ;
Like snow on wool, thy fallings are,
  Soft like a spirit are thy feet.
        Griefs who need fear
        That hath an ear ?
        Down let him lie
        And slumbering die
And change his soul for harmony.

WILLIAM STRODE.

CONTENT.

FROM " PATIENT GRISSEL."

ART thou poor, yet hast thou golden slumbers?
    O sweet content!
Art thou rich, yet is thy mind perplexèd?
    O punishment!
Dost thou laugh to see how fools are vexèd,
To add to golden numbers, golden numbers?
    O sweet content,
      O sweet, O sweet content!
Work apace, apace, apace ;
Honest labor bears a lovely face ;
Then hey nonny nonny, hey nonny nonny.

Canst drink the waters of the crispèd spring ?
    O sweet content!

Swim'st thou in wealth, yet sink'st in thine own
    tears ?
      O punishment!
Then he that patiently want's burden bears,
No burden bears, but is a king, a king,
      O sweet content,
    O sweet, O sweet content!
Work apace, apace, apace ;
Honest labor bears a lovely face ;
Then hey nonny nonny, hey nonny nonny !
                THOMAS DEKKER.

LULLABY.

FROM "PATIENT GRISSEL."

GOLDEN slumbers kiss your eyes,
Smiles awake when you do rise ;
Sleep, pretty wantons ; do not cry,
And I will sing a lullaby,
Rock them, rock them, lullaby.

Care is heavy, therefore sleep you ;
You are care, and care must keep you ;
Sleep, pretty wantons ; do not cry,
And I will sing a lullaby,
Rock them, rock them, lullaby.
                THOMAS DEKKER.

ALL-CONQUERING DEATH.

FROM "THE CONTENTION OF AJAX AND ULYSSES."

THE glories of our blood and state
  Are shadows, not substantial things:
There is no armor against fate,
  Death lays his icy hand on kings:
      Sceptre and crown
      Must tumble down,
And in the dust be equal made
With the poor crooked scythe and spade.

Some men with swords may reap the field,
  And plant fresh laurels where they kill,
But their strong nerves at last must yield,
  They tame but one another still ;
      Early or late,
      They stoop to fate,
And must give up their murmuring breath,
When they, pale captives, creep to death.

The garlands wither on your brow,
  Then boast no more your mighty deeds,
Upon death's purple altar now
  See where the victor-victim bleeds.
      Your hearts must come
      To the cold tomb ;
Only the actions of the just
Smell sweet and blossom in the dust.

JAMES SHIRLEY.

TIME.

FROM "THE AMOROUS WAR."

TIME is a feathered thing,
  And, whilst I praise
  The sparkling of thy looks, and call them ray s,
Takes wing,
Leaving behind him, as he flies,
An unperceivèd dimness in thine eyes.

His minutes whilst they're told,
Do make us old,
And every sand of his fleet glass,
Increasing age as it doth pass,
Insensibly sows wrinkles there,
Where flowers and roses do appear.

Whilst we do speak, our fire
Doth into ice expire ;
  Flames turn to frost,
    And ere we can
    Know how, our crow turns swan,
    Or how, a silver snow
    Springs there, where jet did grow ;
  Our fading spring is in dull winter lost.

JASPER MAYNE.

SILENCE.

STILL-BORN Silence ! thou that art
Flood-gate of the deeper heart !
Offspring of a heavenly kind,
Frost o' the mouth and thaw o' the mind,
Secrecy's confidant, and he
Who makes religion mystery !
Admiration's speaking'st tongue !
Leave thy desert shades among
Reverend hermits' hallowed cells,
Where retired Devotion dwells,
With thy enthusiasms come,
Seize our tongues, and strike us dumb.

RICHARD FLECKNO.

CARES OF STATE.

FROM "ALCIBIADES."

PRINCES that rule, and empires sway,
  How transitory is their state !
Sorrows their glories do allay,
  And richest crowns have greatest weight.

The mighty monarch treason fears,
  Ambitious thoughts within him rave ;
His life all discontent and cares,
  And he at best is but a slave.

Vainly we think with fond delight
  To ease the burden of our cares ;
Each grief a second doth invite,
  And sorrows are each other's heirs.

For me my honor I'll maintain,
  Be gallant, generous, and brave.
But when I quietude would gain,
  At last I find it in the grave.

THOMAS OTWAY.

NATURE'S TRANQUILLITY.

FROM "THE INDIAN EMPEROR."

AH, fading joy; how quickly art thou past!
  Yet we thy ruin haste.
As if the cares of human life were few,
  We seek out new ;
And follow fate, which would too fast pursue.
See, how on every bough the birds express,
  In their sweet notes, their happiness.
  They all enjoy, and nothing spare ;
  But on their mother Nature lay their care ;
Why then should man, the lord of all below,
  Such troubles choose to know,
As none of all his subjects undergo ?

Hark, hark, the waters fall, fall, fall,
And with a murmuring sound
Dash, dash upon the ground,
  To gentle slumbers call.

JOHN DRYDEN.

AGE AND YOUTH.

FROM "THE PASSIONATE PILGRIM."

CRABBED age and youth
  Cannot live together;
Youth is full of pleasance,
  Age is full of care;
Youth like summer morn,
  Age like winter weather:
Youth like summer brave,
  Age like winter bare.

Youth is full of sport;
Age's breath is short,
  Youth is nimble, age is lame;
Youth is hot and bold,
Age is weak and cold;
  Youth is wild, and age is tame.

Age, I do abhor thee;
Youth, I do adore thee;

O, my love, my love is young!
Age, I do defy thee;
O, sweet shepherd, hie thee,
For, methinks, thou stay'st too long.

SHAKESPEARE.

A SONG IN THE PERSON OF WOMANKIND.

MEN, if you love us, play no more
The fools or tyrants with your friends,
To make us still sing o'er and o'er
Our own false praises, for your ends;
We have both wits and fancies too,
And if we must, let 's sing of you.

Nor do we doubt but that we can,
If we would search with care and pain,
Find some one good, in some one man,
So going thorough all your strain.
We shall at last of parcels make
One good enough for a song's sake.

And as a cunning painter takes
In any curious piece you see,
More pleasure while the thing he makes
Than when 'tis made, why, so will we;
And having pleased our art, will try
To make a new, and hang that by.

BEN JONSON.

IN DEFENSE OF INCONSTANCY.

HANG up those dull and envious fools
    That talk abroad of woman's change,
We were not bred to sit on stools,
    Our proper virtue is to range ;
        Take that away, you take our lives.
        We are not women then, but wives.

Such as in valor would excel,
    Do change, though men, and often fight,
Which we in love, must do as well,
    If ever we will love aright ;
        The frequent varying of the deed
        Is that which doth perfection breed.

Nor is't inconstancy to change
    For what is better, as to make,
By searching, what before was strange
    Familiar for the use's sake.
        The good from bad is not descried,
        But as 'tis often vext and tried.

And this profession of a store
    In love, doth not alone help forth
Our pleasure ; but preserves us more
    From being forsaken, than doth worth ;

For were the worthiest woman curst
To love one man, he'd leave her first.

BEN JONSON.

WOMEN ARE MEN'S SHADOWS.

FOLLOW a shadow, it still flies you,
　Seem to fly it, it will pursue ;
So court a mistress, she denies you,
　Let her alone, she will court you :
　　Say, are not woman truly then
　　Styled but the shadows of us men ?

At morn and even shades are longest,
　At noon, they are, or short, or none ;
So men at weakest, they are strongest,
　But grant us perfect, they're not known :
　　Say, are not women truly then
　　Styled but the shadows of us men ?

BEN JONSON.

SONGS OF SORROW.

LAMENT OF PYTHIAS.

FROM "DAMON AND PYTHIAS."

AWAKE! ye woeful wights
    That long have wept in woe :
Resign to me your plaints and tears
  My hapless hap to show.
My woe no tongue can tell,
  No pen can well descry ;
    O what a death is this to hear
    Damon, my friend, must die.

The loss of worldly wealth,
  Man's wisdom may restore,
And physic has provided too
  A salve for every sore ;
But my true friend, once lost,
  No art can well supply ;
    Then what a death is it to hear !
    Damon, my friend, must die.

My mouth refuse the food
  That should my limbs sustain ;
Let sorrow sink into my blood,
  And ransack every vein ;
You furies all at once
  On me your torments try ;
    Why should I live since this I hear, —
    Damon, my friend, must die ?

Gripe me, you greedy griefs,
  And present pangs of death ;
You sisters three, with cruel hands,
  With speed come stop my breath.
Slime me in clay alive,
  Some good man close my eye ;
    O death, come now, seeing I hear
    Damon, my friend, must die.

RICHARD EDWARDS.

ŒNONE'S COMPLAINT.

FROM " THE ARRAIGNMENT OF PARIS."

MELPOMONE, the muse of tragic songs,
With mournful tunes, in stole of dismal hue,
Assist a silly nymph to wail her woe,
And leave thy lusty company behind.

Thou luckless wreath ! becomes me not to wear
The poplar tree, for triumph of my love ;

Then as my joy, my pride of love is left,
Be thou unclothèd of thy lovely green.

And in thy leaves my future written be,
And them some gentle wind let blow abroad,
That all the world may see how false of love,
False Paris has to his Œnone been.

GEORGE PEELE.

SEPHESTIA'S SONG TO HER CHILD.

FROM " MENAPHON."

WEEP not, my wanton, smile upon my knee,
When thou art old, there's grief enough for thee !
      Mother's wag, pretty boy,
      Father's sorrow, father's joy !
      When thy father first did see
      Such a boy by him and me,
      He was glad, I was woe,
      Fortune's change'd made him so ;
      When he had left his pretty boy,
      Last his sorrow, first his joy ;

Weep not, my wanton, smile upon my knee,
When thou art old, there's grief enough for thee !
      Streaming tears that never stint,
      Like pearl-drops from a flint,

Fell by course from his eyes
That one another's place supplies ;
Thus he grieved in every part,
Tears of blood fell from his heart
When he left his pretty boy,
Father's sorrow, father's joy.

Weep not, my wanton, smile upon my knee,
When thou art old, there's grief enough for thee.

The wanton smiled, father wept,
Mother cried, baby leapt,
More thou crowed, more he cried,
Nature could not sorrow hide ;
He must go, he must kiss
Child and mother, baby bless ;
For he left his pretty boy,
Father's sorrow, father's joy.

Weep not, my wanton, smile upon my knee,
When thou art old, there's grief enough for thee !

ROBERT GREENE.

COME, DEATH.

FROM "TWELFTH NIGHT."

COME away, come away, Death,
And in sad cypress let me be laid ;
Fly away, fly away, breath,
I am slain by a fair, cruel maid.

My shroud of white, stuck all with yew,
    O prepare it!
My part of death, no one so true
    Did share it.

  Not a flower, not a flower sweet
On my black coffin let there be strown;
  Not a friend, not a friend greet
My poor corpse, where my bones shall be thrown:
A hundred thousand sighs to save,
    Lay me, O, where
Sad true lover ne'er find my grave,
    To weep there.

                 SHAKESPEARE.

ASPATIA'S SONG.

FROM "THE MAID'S TRAGEDY."

LAY a garland on my hearse
    Of the dismal yew;
Maidens, willow branches bear,
    Say I died true.

My love was false, but I was firm
    From my hour of birth;
Upon my buried body lie
    Lightly, gentle earth.

          BEAUMONT AND FLETCHER.

9

DIRGE AT HERO'S TOMB.

FROM " MUCH ADO ABOUT NOTHING."

PARDON, goddess of the night,
Those that slew thy virgin knight ;
For the which, with songs of woe,
Round about her tomb they go.
  Midnight, assist our moan ;
  Help us to sigh and groan,
      Heavily, heavily ;
  Graves yawn, and yield your dead,
  Till death be utterèd,
      Heavily, heavily.

SHAKESPEARE.

DIRGE FOR IMOGEN.

FROM "CYMBELINE."

FEAR no more the heat o' the sun,
  Nor the furious winter's rages ;
Thou thy worldly task has done,
  Home art gone, and ta'en thy wages :
Golden lads and girls all must,
Like chimney-sweepers, come to dust.

Fear no more the frown o' the great ;
  Thou art past the tyrant's stroke ;

Care no more to clothe and eat ;
To thee the reed is as the oak :
The sceptre, learning, physic, must
All follow this, and come to dust.

Fear no more the lightning flash,
Nor th' all dreaded thunder-stone ;
Fear not slander, censure rash ;
Thou hast finished joy and moan :
All lovers young, all lovers must
Consign to thee, and come to dust.

No exorciser harm thee !
Nor no witchcraft charm thee !
Ghost unlaid forbear thee !
Nothing ill come near thee !
Quiet consummation have ;
And renowned be thy grave !

SHAKESPEARE.

ECHO'S PLAINT.

FROM "CYNTHIA'S REVELS."

SLOW, slow, fresh fount, keep time with my salt tears ;
Yet, slower yet ; O faintly, gentle springs ;
List to the heavy past the music bears,
Woe weeps out her division, when she sings.
Drop herbs and flowers,
Fall grief in showers :

Our beauties are not ours.
O, I could still,
Like melting snow upon some craggy hill,
Drop, drop, drop, drop,
Since Nature's pride is now a withered daffodil.

BEN JONSON.

LAMENT.

FROM "THE CAPTAIN."

AWAY, delights! go seek some other dwelling,
For I must die.
Farewell, false Love! thy tongue is ever telling
Lie after lie.
Forever let me rest now, from thy smarts;
Alas, for pity go,
And fire their hearts
That have been hard to thee! mine was not so!

Never again deluding love shall know me,
For I will die,
And all those griefs that think to overgrow me,
Shall be as I;
Forever will I sleep, while poor maids cry, —
"Alas, for pity, stay
And let us die
With thee! men cannot mock us in the clay."

BEAUMONT AND FLETCHER.

BURIAL DIRGE.

FROM "THE TWO NOBLE KINSMEN."

URNS and odors bring away,
Vapors, sighs, darken the day !
Our dole more deadly looks than dying !
Balms, and gums, and heavy cheers,
Sacred vials filled with tears,
And clamors, through the mild air flying ;
Come, all sad and solemn shows,
That are quick-eyed Pleasure's foes !
We convent with naught but woes,
We convent with naught but woes.

BEAUMONT AND FLETCHER.

MARCELLO'S BURIAL DIRGE.

FROM "THE WHITE DEVIL."

CALL for the robin-redbreast and wren,
Since o'er shady groves they hover,
And with leaves and flowers do cover
The friendless bodies of unburied men.

Call unto his funeral dole
The ant, the field-mouse, and the mole,
To raise him hillocks that shall keep him warm,
And, when gay tombs are robbed, sustain no harm.

But keep the wolf far hence that's foe to men,
For with his nails he'll dig them up again.

JOHN WEBSTER.

DEATH-WATCH.

FROM "THE DUCHESS OF MALFY."

HARK! now everything is still,
The screech-owl, and the whistler shrill,
Call upon our dame aloud,
And bid her quickly don her shroud.

Much you had of land and rent,
Your length in clay's now competent;
A long war disturbed your mind,
Here your perfect peace is signed.

Of what is't fools make such vain keeping
Sin, their conception; their birth, weeping;
Their life, a general mist of error;
Their death, a hideous storm of terror.

Strew your hair with powders sweet,
Don clean linen, bathe your feet,
And the foul fiend more to check,
A crucifix let bless your neck.

'Tis now full tide 'tween night and day,
End your groan, and come away.

JOHN WEBSTER.

SONGS.

FROM " THE BROKEN HEART."

I.

O, no more, no more, too late
  Sighs are spent ; the burning tapers
Of a life as chaste as fate,
  Pure as are unwritten papers,
Are burnt out ; no heat, no light
Now remains ; 'tis even night.
  Love is dead ; let lover's eyes
      Locked in endless dreams,
      Th' extreme of all extremes,
  Ope no more, for now love dies,
Now love dies,— implying,
Love's martyrs must be ever, ever dying.

II.

Glories, pleasures, pomps, delights, and ease,
      Can but please
The outward sense, when the mind
Is not untroubled, or by peace refined ;
Crowns may flourish and decay,
Beauties shine, but fade away ;
Youth may revel, but it must
Lie down in a bed of dust ;
Earthly honors flow and waste
Time alone doth change and last.

Sorrows, mingled with contents, prepare
Rest from care ;
Love only reigns in death, though art
Can find no comfort for a broken heart.

JOHN FORD.

LONGING FOR DEATH.

FROM "THE EMPEROR OF THE EAST."

WHY art thou slow, thou rest of trouble, Death,
To stop a wretch's breath ?
That calls on thee, and offers her sad heart,
.   A prey unto thy dart.
I am nor young nor fair ; be therefore bold ;
Sorrow hath made me old,
Deformed, and wrinkled ; all that I can crave,
Is quiet in my grave.
Such as live happy, hold long life a jewel ;
But to me thou art cruel,
If thou end not my tedious misery,
And I soon cease to be.
Strike, and strike home, then ; pity unto me,
In one short hour's delay, is tyranny.

PHILIP MASSINGER.

COMIC SONGS

AND

SONGS OF CLOWNS.

———•———

CLOWN'S SONGS.

FROM "TWELFTH NIGHT."

I.

O MISTRESS mine, where are you roaming?
 O stay and hear; your true love's coming,
  That can sing both high and low:
Trip no further, pretty sweeting;
Journeys end in lovers meeting,
  Every wise man's son does know.

What is love? 'tis not hereafter;
Present mirth hath present laughter;
  What's to come, is still unsure:
In delay there lies no plenty;
Then come and kiss me, sweet and twenty,
  Youth's a stuff will not endure.

II.

When that I was and a tiny little boy,
　With hey, ho, the wind and the rain,
A foolish thing was but a toy,
　For the rain it raineth every day.

But when I came to man's estate,
　With hey, ho, the wind and the rain,
'Gainst knaves and thieves men shut the gate,
　For the rain it raineth every day.

But when I came at last to wive,
　With hey, ho, the wind and the rain,
By swaggering I could never thrive,
　For the rain it raineth every day.

But when I came unto my bed,
　With hey, ho, the wind and the rain,
The toss-pots still had drunken head,
　For the rain it raineth every day.

A great while ago the world begun,
　With hey, ho, the wind and the rain,
But that's all one, our play's all done,
　And the rain it raineth every day.

SHAKESPEARE.

SONGS OF AUTOLYCUS.

FROM " THE WINTER'S TALE."

WHEN daffodils begin to peer, —
  With heigh ! the doxy over the dale, —
Why, then comes .in the sweet o' the year,
  For the red blood reigns in the winter's pale.

The white sheet bleaching on the hedge, —
  With heigh ! the sweet birds, O, how they sing, ·
Doth set my pugging tooth on edge,
  For a quart of ale is a dish for a king.

The lark that tirra-lira chants, —
  With heigh ! with heigh ! the thrush and the jay, —
Are summer songs for me and my aunts,
  As we lie tumbling in the hay.

(*Speaking.*)   I have served Prince Florizel, and in my
time worn three-pile, and now I out of service.

(*Sings.*) But shall I go mourn for that, my dear,
      The moon doth shine by night,
   And when I wander here and there,
      I then do most go right.

   If tinkers may have leave to live,
      And bear the sow-skin bowget,

Then my account I well may give,
    And in the stocks avouch it.

Jog on, jog on, the footpath way,
    And merrily hint the stile-a ;
A merry heart goes all the day,
    Your sad one tires in a mile-a.

II.

(*Autolycus, as a peddler.*)

Lawn, as white as driven snow,
Cyprus, black as e'er was crow ;
Gloves, as sweet as damask roses ;
Masks for faces, and for noses ;
Bugle-bracelet, necklace-amber ;
Perfume for a lady's chamber ;
Golden quoifs and stomachers,
For my lads to give their dears ;
Pins, and poking-sticks of steel,
What maids lack from head to heel :
Come, buy of me, come ; come buy, come buy,
Buy lads, or else your lasses cry ; come buy.

Will you buy any tape,
Or lace for your cape,
    My dainty duck, my dear-a ?
Any silk, any thread,
Any toys for your head,

Of the new'st, and fin'st, fin'st wear-a ?
　　Come to the peddler,
　　Money 's a meddler
That doth utter all men's ware-a.

SHAKESPEARE.

THE FOOL.

FROM " VOLPONE."

FOOLS, they are the only nation
Worth men's envy or admiration ;
Free from care, or sorrow-taking,
Selves and others merry-making ;
All they say or do is sterling,
Your fool, he is your great man's darling,
And your ladies' sport and pleasure,
Tongue and bauble are his treasure ;
E'en his face begetteth laughter,
And he speaks truth free from slaughter ;
He 's the grace of every feast ;
And sometimes the chiefest guest
Hath his trencher and his stool,
When wit waits upon the fool.
　　　O, who would be
　　　He, he, he ?

BEN JONSON.

MERRYTHOUGHT'S SONG.

FROM "THE KNIGHTS OF THE BURNING PESTLE."

FOR Jillian of Berry, she dwells on a hill,
And she hath good beer and ale to sell,
And of good fellows she thinks no ill:
And thither will we go now, now, now,
    And thither will we go now.

And when you have made a little stay,
You need not ask what is to pay,
But kiss your hostess and go your way:
And thither will we go now, now, now,
    And thither will we go now.

                BEAUMONT AND FLETCHER.

BACCHANALIAN SONGS.

JOLLY GOOD ALE AND OLD.

FROM "GAMMER GURTON'S NEEDLE."

I CANNOT eat but little meat,
    My stomach is not good ;
But sure, I think that I can drink
    With him that wears a hood.
Though I go bare, take ye no care,
    I am nothing a cold,
I stuff my skin so full within,
    Of jolly good ale and old.
Back and side go bare, go bare,
    Both foot and hand go cold ;
But belly, God send thee good ale enough,
    Whether it be new or old.

I have no roast, but a nut-brown toast,
    And a crab laid in the fire ;
A little bread, shall do me stead,
    Much bread I not desire :

No frost, nor snow, no wind, I trow,
    Can hurt me if I wold,
I am so wrapt and thoroughly lapt
    In jolly good ale and old.
Back and side go bare, go bare,
    Both foot and hand go cold ;
But belly, God send thee good ale enough,
    Whether it be new or old.

And Tib, my wife, that as her life
    Loveth well good ale to seek,
Full oft drinks she, till you may see
    The tears run down her cheek ;
Then doth she trowl to me the bowl,
    Even as a maltworm should,
And saith, " Sweetheart, I took my part
    Of this jolly old ale and good."
Back and side go bare, go bare,
    Both foot and hand go cold ;
But belly, God send thee good ale enough,
    Whether it be new or old.

Now let them drink, till they nod and wink,
    Even as good fellows should do ;
They shall not miss to have the bliss
    Good ale doth bring men to :
And all poor souls that have scourèd bowls,
    Or have them lustily trowled ;

God save the lives of them and their wives,
  Whether they be young or old.
Back and side go bare, go bare,
  Both foot and hand go cold ;
But belly, God send thee good ale enough,
  Whether it be new or old.

JOHN STILL.

INVOCATION TO BACCHUS.

FROM "ANTONY AND CLEOPATRA."

COME, thou monarch of the vine,
Plumpy Bacchus with pink eyne!
In thy vats our cares be drowned,
With thy grapes our hairs be crowned:
Cup us, till the world go round,
Cup us, till the world go round!

SHAKESPEARE.

FESTIVE SONG.

FROM "THE POETASTER."

WAKE ! our mirth begins to die,
  Quicken it with tunes and wine ;
Raise your notes ; you're out, fie ! fie !
  This drowsiness is an ill sign.
  We banish him the quire of gods
10

That droops again :
Then all are men,
For here's not one but nods.

Then in a free and lofty strain,
  Our broken tunes we thus repair,
And we answer them again,
    Running division on the panting air.
    To celebrate this feast of sense,
    As free from scandal as offense.
  Here is beauty for the eye,
  For the ear sweet melody,
Ambrosial odors for the smell,
  Delicious nectar for the taste,
  For the touch, a lady's waist,
Which doth all the rest excel.

BEN JONSON.

TO COMUS.

FROM " A MASQUE BEFORE KING JAMES."

ROOM ! room ! make room for the bouncing belly,
First father of sauce, and deviser of jelly ;
Prime master of arts, and the giver of wit,
That found out that excellent engine, the spit ;
The plough and the flail, the hill and the hopper,
The hutch and the boulter, the furnace and copper,
The oven, the bavin, the mawkin, the peel,
The hearth and the range, the dog and the wheel.

He, he first invented the hogshead and tun,
The gimlet and vice too, and taught them to run ;
And since, with the funnel and Hippocras' bag,
He has made of himself, that now he cries swag ;
Which shows, though the pleasure be but of four inches,
Yet he is a weasel, the gullet that pinches
Of any delight, and not spares from his back
Whatever, to make of the belly a sack.

Hail, hail, plump paunch ! O the founder of taste !
For fresh meats or powdered, or pickle, or paste ;
Devourer of broiled, baked, roasted, or sod,
And emptier of cups, be they even or odd ;
All which have now made thee so wide in the waist,
As scarce with no pudding thou art to be laced ;
But eating and drinking until thou dost nod,
Thou break'st all thy girdles, and breaks forth a god.

BEN JONSON.

TO BACCHUS.

FROM " VALENTINIAN."

GOD Lyæus, ever young,
Ever honored, ever sung,
Stained with blood of lusty grapes ;
In a thousand lusty shapes
Dance upon the mazer's brim —
In the crimson liquor swim :

From thy plenteous hand divine,
Let a river run with wine;
　　God of youth, let this day here
　　Enter neither care nor fear!

BEAUMONT AND FLETCHER.

DRINK, BOYS, DRINK!

FROM " THE BLOODY BROTHER."

DRINK to-day, and drown all sorrow,
You will, perhaps, not do it to-morrow;
Best, while you have it, use your breath,
There is no drinking after death.

Wine works the heart up, wakes the wit,
There is no cure 'gainst age but it;
It helps the headache, cough, and phthisic,
And is for all diseases physic.

Then let us swill, boys, for your health,
Who drinks well, loves the commonwealth;
And he that will to bed go sober,
Falls with the leaf, still in October.

BEAUMONT AND FLETCHER.

CAMP SONG.

FROM "THE KNIGHTS OF MALTA."

SIT, soldiers, sit and sing, the round is clear,
And cock-a-loodle-loo tells us the day is near ;
Each toss his can, until his throat be mellow, —
Drink, laugh, and sing ! the soldier has no fellow.

To thee a full pot, my little lance prisado,
And when thou hast done a pipe of Trinidado ;
Our glass of life runs wine, the vintner skinks it,
Whilst with his wife the frolic soldier drinks it.

The drums beat, ensigns wave, and cannons thump it,
Our game is ruffe, and the best heart doth trump it ;
Each toss his can, until his throat be mellow, —
Drink, laugh, and sing ! the soldier has no fellow.

I'll pledge thee, my corporal, were it a flagon.
After, watch fiercer than George did the dragon ;
What blood we lose i' the town, we gain i' the tuns ;
Furred gowns, and flat caps, give the wall to guns ;
Each toss his can, until his throat be mellow, —
Drink, laugh, and sing ! the soldier has no fellow.

BEAUMONT AND FLETCHER.

THE JOVIAL PHILOSOPHER.

FROM " WHAT YOU WILL."

Music, tobacco, sack, and sleep,
The tide of sorrow backward keep ;
If thou art sad at others' fate,
Riva, drink deep, give care the mate.

On us the end of time is come,
Fond fear of that we cannot shun ;
Whilst quickest sense doth freshly last,
Clip time about, hug pleasure fast.

The sisters ravel out our twine ;
He that knows little's most divine ;
Error deludes ; who'll beat this hence,
Naught's known but by exterior sense.

Let glory blazon others' deed,
My blood, than breath, craves better meed ;
Let twattling fame cheat others' rest,
I am no dish for Rumor's feast.

Let honor others' hope abuse,
I'll nothing have, so naught will lose ;
I'll strive to be, nor great, nor small,
To live, nor die ; fate helmeth all ;

When I can breathe no longer, then,
Heaven take all, there put Amen!

JOHN MARSTON.

SONG.

FROM "THE SUN'S DARLING."

CAST away care; for he that loves sorrow,
Nor lengthens to-day, nor can buy him to-morrow,
Money is trash, and he that will spend it,
Let him drink merrily, fortune will send it.
    Merrily, merrily, O! ho! ho!
    Play it off stiffly, we may not part so.

Wine is a charm, it gives heat to the blood,
And the coward is armed, if his liquor be good;
Wine quickens the wit, and makes the back able,
And it scorns to submit to the watch or constable.
    Merrily, merrily, O! ho! ho!
    Play it off stiffly, we may not part so.

Let the pots fly about, give us more liquor,
Our wits will be nimbler, our brains will be quicker;
Empty the cask and score up, we care not,
Fill the pots all again, drink on, and spare not.
    Merrily, merrily, O! ho! ho!
    Play it off stiffly, we may not part so.

JOHN FORD.

THE PRAISE OF OLD SACK.

FROM "ARISTIPPUS."

WE care not for money, riches, nor wealth ;
Old sack is our money, old sack is our wealth ;
　　　　Then let's flock hither,
　　　　Like birds of a feather,
To drink, to fling,
To laugh, and sing,
　　　　　　Conferring our notes together,
　　　　　　Conferring our notes together.

Come let us laugh, let us drink, let us sing.
The winter with us is good as the spring ;
　　　　We care not a feather
　　　　For wind or weather,
But night and day,
We sport and play,
　　　　　　Conferring our notes together,
　　　　　　Conferring our notes together.
　　　　　　　　　　THOMAS RANDOLPH.

THE EPICURE.

ANACREONTIC.

FILL the bowl with rosy wine,
Around our temples roses twine ;

And let us cheerfully awhile,
Like the wine and roses, smile.
Crowned with roses, we contemn
Gyge's wealthy diadem.

To-day is ours; what do we fear?
To-day is ours; we have it here:
Let's treat it kindly, that it may
Wish, at least, with us to stay;
Let's banish business, banish sorrow;
To the gods belong to-morrow.

ABRAHAM COWLEY.

SONGS OF FAIRIES AND SPIRITS.

. CHORUS OF WITCHES.

FROM "THE WITCH."

Chorus of spirits in the air.   COME away, come away,
        Hecate, Hecate, come away.
Hecate.   I come, I come, I come,
        With all the speed I may,
        With all the speed I may.
        Where's Stadlin ?
Chorus.   Here.
Hecate.   Where's Puckle ?   ·
Chorus.   Here.
        And Hoppo too, and Hellwain too.
        We lack but you, we lack but you ;
        Come away, make up the count.
Hecate.   I will but noint, and then I'll mount. [*She ascends.*
        Now I go, now I fly,
        Malkin, my sweet spirit, and I.

O what a dainty pleasure 'tis
To ride in the air, when the moon shines fair,
And sing, and dance, and toy, and kiss !
Over woods, high rocks, and mountains ;
Over seas, our mistress' fountains ;
Over steep towers and turrets
We fly by night 'mongst troops of spirits.
No ring of bells to our ears sounds,
No howl of wolves, no yelp of hounds ;
No, not the noise of waters' breach,
Or cannon's roar, our height can reach.

Chorus repeat.   No ring of bells, etc.

JOHN MIDDLETON.

SONGS OF ARIEL.

FROM " THE TEMPEST."

I.

COME unto these yellow sands,
And then take hands :
Court'sied when you have and kist
The wild waves whist,
Foot it featly here and there ;
And, sweet sprites, the burden bear.
Hark, hark !
Burden.   Bough, wough !

The watch-dogs bark:
  Bough, wough!
Hark, hark! I hear
The strain of strutting chanticleer
Cry, Cock-a-diddle-dow.

II.

Full fadom five thy father lies;
  Of his bones are coral made;
Those are pearls that were his eyes:
  Nothing of him that doth fade
But doth suffer a sea-change
Into something rich and strange.
Sea-nymphs hourly ring his knell:
                    Ding-dong.
Hark! now I hear them, Ding-dong, bell!

III.

Where the bee sucks, there suck I:
  In a cowslip's bell I lie;
There I couch when owls do cry.
  On the bat's back I do fly
  After summer merrily.
  Merrily, merrily, shall I live now
Under the blossom that hangs on the bough.

                    SHAKESPEARE.

FAIRIES' SONG.

FROM "THE MERRY WIVES OF WINDSOR."

Fye on sinful fantasy!
Fye on lust and luxury!
Lust is but a bloody fire,
Kindled with unchaste desire,   '
Fed in heart, whose flames aspire
As thoughts do blow them, higher and higher.
Pinch him, fairies, mutually;
Pinch him for his villainy;
Pinch him, and burn him, and turn him about,
Till candles and starlight and moonshine be out.

SHAKESPEARE.

TITANIA'S LULLABY.

FROM "A MIDSUMMER-NIGHT'S DREAM."

You spotted snakes, with double tongue,
  Thorny hedgehogs, be not seen;
Newts, and blind-worms, do no wrong,
  Come not near our Fairy Queen.
  Philomel, with melody
  Sing in our sweet lullaby:
Lulla, lulla, lullaby; lulla, lulla, lullaby:
  Never harm, nor spell, nor charm,
  Come our lovely lady nigh;
  So good-night, with lullaby.

Weaving spiders come not here;
　Hence, you long-legged spinners, hence!
Beetles black, approach not near;
　Worm, nor snail, do no offense.
　Philomel, with melody
　Sing in our sweet lullaby:
Lulla, lulla, lullaby; lulla, lulla, lullaby:
　Never harm, nor spell, nor charm,
　Come our lovely lady nigh;
　So good-night, with lullaby.

SHAKESPEARE.

FAY'S SONG.

FROM "A MIDSUMMER-NIGHT'S DREAM."

OVER hill, over dale,
　Thorough bush, thorough brier,
Over park, over pale,
　Thorough flood, thorough fire,
I do wander everywhere,
Swifter than the moon's sphere;
And I serve the Fairy Queen,
To dew her orbs upon the green.
The cowslips tall her pensioners be:
In their gold coats spots you see;
Those be rubies, fairy favors,
In those freckles live their savors:
I must go seek some dewdrops here,
And hang a pearl in every cowslip's ear.

SHAKESPEARE.

PUCK'S SONG — MIDNIGHT.

FROM " A MIDSUMMER-NIGHT'S DREAM."

Now the hungry lion roars,
  And the wolf behowls the moon ;
Whilst the heavy ploughman snores,
  All with weary task fordone.
Now the wasted brands do glow,
  Whilst the screech-owl, screeching loud,
Puts the wretch that lies in woe
  In remembrance of a shroud.
Now it is the time of night
  That the graves, all gaping wide,
Every one lets forth his sprite,
  In the church-way paths to glide :
And we fairies, that do run
  By the triple Hecate's team,
From the presence of the sun,
  Following darkness like a dream,
Now we frolic : not a mouse
Shall disturb this hallowed house :
I am sent with broom before,
To sweep the dust behind the door.

SHAKESPEARE.

WITCH'S CONJURATION TO ATE.

FROM "THE MASQUE OF QUEENS."

1*st Charm.*   DAME, dame, the watch is set ;
                Quickly come ; we all are met, — ✓
                From the lakes, and from the fens,
                From the rocks, and from the dens,
                From the woods, and from the caves,
                From the churchyard, from the graves,
                From the dungeon, from the tree
                That they die on : here are we.

2*d Charm.*   The weather is fair, the wind is good,
                Up dame, on your horse of wood ;
                Or else tuck up your gray frock,
                And saddle your goat, or your green cock,
                And make his bridle a bottom of thread,
                To roll up how many miles you have rid.
                    Quickly come away,
                    For we all stay.

3*d Charm.*   The owl is abroad, the bat, and the toad,
                And so is the cat-a-mountain ;
            The ant and the mole sit both in a hole,
                And the frog peeps out of the fountain ;
            The dogs they do bay, and the timbrels play,
                The spindle is now a-turning ;   .

11   .

The moon it is red, and the stars are fled,
 But all the sky is a-burning ;
The ditch is made, and our nails the spade ;
 With pictures full of wax and wool,
Their livers I stick, with needles quick ;
 There lacks but the blood, to make up the flood :
Quickly, dame, then bring your part in,
 Spur, spur, upon little Martin.

4th Charm. Deep, O deep we lay thee to sleep,
We leave thee drink by, if thou chance to be dry,
Both milk and blood, the dew and the flood.
We breathe in thy bed at the foot and the head,
We cover thee warm, that thou take no harm ;
   And when thou dost wake,
   Dame Earth shall quake,
   And the houses shake.

5th Charm. The sticks are across, there can be no loss,
The sage is rotten, the sulphur is gotten :
Up to the sky that was in the ground,
Follow it then with our rattles round
Under the bramble, over the brier,
A little more heat will set it on fire ;
Put it in mind to do it kind,
Flow water and blow wind,
Rouncy is over, Robble is under ;
A flash of light and a clap of thunder,

A storm of rain, another of hail,
We all must home in the egg-shell sail :
The mast is made of a great pin,
The tackle of cobweb, the sail as thin,
And if we go through and not fall in —

6th Charm. Bark dogs, wolves howl,
    Seas roar, woods roll,
    Clouds crack, all be black
    But the light our charms do make.

7th Charm. A cloud of pitch, a spur and a switch,
    To haste him away, and a whirlwind play
    Before and after, with thunder for laughter,
    And storms for joy of the roaring boy ;
    His head of a drake, his tail of a snake.

8th Charm. About, about, and about,
    Till the mists arise, and the lights fly out,
    The images neither be seen nor felt ;
    The woolen burn, and the waxen melt :
    Sprinkle your liquors upon the ground,
    And into the air ; around, around,
        Around, around,
        Till a music sound,
        And a pace be found
        To which we may dance,
        And our charms advance.

BEN JONSON.

TO CYNTHIA.

FROM " CYNTHIA'S REVELS."

QUEEN and huntress, chaste and fair,
　Now the sun is laid to sleep,
Seated in thy silver car,
　State in wonted manner keep:
　　　Hesperus entreats thy light,
　　　Goddess excellently bright.

Earth, let not thy envious shade
　Dare itself to interpose ;
Cynthia's shining orb was made
　Heaven to clear when day did close.
　　　Bless us, then, with wishèd light,
　　　Goddess excellently bright.

Lay thy bow of pearl apart,
　And thy crystal-shining quiver ;
Give unto the flying hart
　Space to breathe, how short soever,
　　　Thou that mak'st a day of night,
　　　Goddess excellently bright.

' BEN JONSON.

SONGS.

I.

(*Comus sings.*)

THE star that bids the shepherd fold,
Now the top of heaven doth hold ;
And the gilded car of day
His glowing axle doth allay
In the steep Atlantic stream ;
And the slope sun his upward beam
Shoots against the dusky pole,
Pacing towards the other goal
Of his chamber in the east.
Meanwhile, welcome, Joy and Feast,
Midnight shout and Revelry,
Tipsy Dance and Jollity.
Braid your locks with rosy twine,
Dropping odors, dropping wine :
Rigor now is gone to bed,
And Advice, with scrupulous head,
Strict Age and sour Severity,
With their grave saws in slumber lie.
We that are of purer fire
Imitate the starry quire
Who in their nightly watchful spheres,
Lead in swift round the months and years.

The sounds and seas, with all their finny drove,
Now to the moon in wavering morrice move,
And on the tawny sands and shelves,
Trip the pert fairies and the dapper elves.
By dimpled brook and fountain's brim
The wood-nymphs, decked with daisies trim,
Their merry wakes and pastimes keep ;
What hath night to do with sleep ?
Night hath better sweets to prove,
Venus now wakes, and wakens love.
Come, let us our rites begin,
'Tis only daylight that makes sin,
Which these dun shades will ne'er report.
Hail, goddess of nocturnal sport,
Dark-veiled Cotytto ! t'whom the secret flame
Of midnight torches burns ; mysterious dame,
That ne'er art called but when the dragon womb
Of Stygian darkness spots her thickest gloom
And makes one blot of all the air,
Stay thy cloudy ebon chair,
Wherein thou rid'st with Hecate, and befriend
Us, thy vowed priests, till utmost end
Of all thy dues be done, and none left out,
Ere the babbling eastern scout,
The nice morn, on th' Indian steep,
From her cabined loop-hole peep,
And to the tell-tale sun descry
Our concealed solemnity.

Come, knit hands, and beat the ground
In a light fantastic round.

II.

TO ECHO.

Sweet Echo, sweetest nymph, that liv'st unseen
   Within thy airy shell
By slow Meander's margent green,
And in the violet embroidered dell,
   Where the love-lorn nightingale
Nightly to thee her sad song mourneth well,
Can'st thou not tell me of a gentle pair
   That likest thy Narcissus are ?
   Or, if thou have
   Hid them in some flowery cave,
   Tell me but where.
Sweet queen of parly, daughter of the sphere,
So mayst thou be translated to the skies,
And give resounding grace to all heaven's harmonies !

III.

INVOCATION TO THE GODDESS OF THE SEVERN.

(*Spirit sings.*)

  Sabrina fair,
 Listen where thou art sitting,
Under the glassy, cool, translucent wave,
 In twisted braids of lilies knitting

The loose train of thy amber-dropping hair.
.Listen for dear honor's sake :
Goddess of the silver lake,
Listen and save.

Listen and appear to us,
In name of great Oceanus :
By the earth-shaking Neptune's mace,
And Tethy's grave majestic pace ;
By hoary Nereus' wrinkled look,
And the Carpathian's wizard's hook ;
By scaly Triton's winding shell,
And old soothsaying Glaucus' spell ;
By Leucothea's lovely hands,
And by her son that rules the strands ;
By Thetis' tinsel-slippered feet,
And the songs of sirens sweet ;
By dead Parthenope's dear tomb,
And fair Ligea's golden comb,
Wherewith she sits on diamond rocks,
Sleeking her soft alluring locks ;
By all the nymphs that nightly dance
Upon thy streams, with wily glance, —
Rise, rise, and heave thy rosy head
From thy coral-paven bed,
And bridle in thy head-long wave,
Till thou our summons answered have.

IV.

SABRINA'S ANSWER.

By the rushy-fringèd bank,
Where grows the willow and the osier dank,
   My sliding chariot stays,
Thick-set with agate, and the azure sheen
Of turkis blue and emerald green
   That in the channel strays,
Whilst from off the waters fleet
Thus I set my printless feet
O'er the cowslip's velvet head   .
That bends not at my tread:
Gentle swain, at thy request,
   I am here.

V.

FAREWELL SONG OF THE SPIRIT.

To the ocean now I fly,
And those happy climes that lie
Where day never shuts his eye,
Up in the broad fields of the sky;

There I suck the liquid air,
All amidst the gardens fair
Of Hesperus, and his daughters three
That sing about the golden tree.

Along the crispèd shades and bowers
Revels the spruce and jocund Spring :
The Graces and the rosy-bosomed Hours
Thither all their bounties bring.

There eternal Summer dwells,
And west winds, with murky wing,
About the cedarn alleys fling
Nard and cassia's balmy smells.

Iris there with humid bow
Waters the odorous banks that blow
Flowers of more unmingled hue
Than her purpled scarf can show,
And drenches with Elysian dew
(List, mortals, if your ears be true)
Beds of hyacinth and roses
Where young Adonis oft reposes,
Waxing well of his deep wound
In slumber soft ; and on the ground
Sadly sits the Assyrian queen :
But far above, in tangled sheen,
Celestial Cupid, her famed son, advanced,
Holds his dear Psyche sweet entranced,
After her wand'ring labors long,
Till free consent the gods among,
Make her his eternal bride ;
And from her pure unspotted side,

Two blissful twins are to be born,
Youth and Joy ; so Jove hath sworn.

But now my task is smoothly done,
I can fly, or I can run
Quickly to the green earth's end,
Where the bowed welkin slow doth bend :
And from thence can soar as soon
To the corners of the moon.

Mortals that would follow me,
Love Virtue, she alone is free ;
She can teach you how to climb
Higher than the sphery chime :
Or if Virtue feeble were,
Heaven itself would stoop to her.

JOHN MILTON.

INCANTATION.

FROM " ŒDIPUS."

CHOOSE the darkest part o' th' grove,
Such as ghosts at noonday love.
Dig a trench, and dig it nigh
Where the bones of Laius lie :
Altars raised of turf or stone,
Will th' infernal powers have none,
Answer me, if this be done ?

Chorus.   'Tis done.

Is the sacrifice made fit?
Draw her backward to the pit:
Draw the barren heifer back;
Barren let her be, and black.
Cut the curled hair that grows
Full betwixt her horns and brows,
And turn your faces from the sun.
Answer me, if this be done?

Chorus   'Tis done.

Pour in blood, and blood, like wine,
To mother Earth and Proserpine;
Mingle milk into the stream;
Feast the ghosts that love the steam;
Snatch a brand from funeral pile;
Toss it in to make it boil;
And turn your faces from the sun.
Answer me, if this be done?

Chorus.   'Tis done.

JOHN DRYDEN.

NOTES.

———◆———

PAGE 3, line 2. — *Will Somers*, or Summers, was a jester of note who was a favorite at the court of Henry VIII. (See Arnim's "Nest of Ninnies.") The play of Nash's which bears his name was first performed in a barn in the country during the prevalence of the plague in London.

Page 22, line 4. — *Arcades*. Milton's name does not strictly belong among the old dramatists. He has earned his place among them as much by his defense of Tragedy in the preface to "Sampson Agonistes," as by that noble tragedy itself, if we regard it merely in its adaptedness for representation. His two masques, however, "Comus" and "Arcades," were both represented on the public stage. Of these spectacles, so frequent in the reigns of Elizabeth and James I., and many of them containing some of the finest specimens of imaginative poetry in the language, "Comus" stands among the first. "Arcades," although much less familiar to the general reader, has many of the characteristic beauties of the poet.

Page 24, 2d line from bottom. — These lines from Milton suggest that —
> "Such harmony is in immortal souls —
> But, whilst this muddy vesture of decay
> Doth grossly close in, we cannot hear it."
> — *Merchant of Venice.*

Page 28, line 6. — Richard Brome was at one time a servant of Ben Jonson. It is possible that an old mantle of the master may have descended upon the shoulders of the valet, at all events, after leaving his service he wrote fifteen plays, of which the titles are preserved, and all of which were performed. Brome was the "son" of Dekker in the same manner as Shirley was adopted by Chapman, Field by Massinger, and Randolph, and afterwards Cartwright, by Jonson. It is not quite clear what was the nature of this literary adoption, but it is pleasing to contemplate in imagination the paternal relation on the part of a distinguished poet, towards his young and unfledged protégé.

Page 30, line 15. — Dyce says it should be printed " pretty *is*," and that Hanmer first read *bin* for the rhyme. It is hard to give up the rhyme we have heard so long, and therefore I have written it *bin.*

Page 37, line 1. — *Cupid and Campaspe.* The play of " Alexander and Campaspe " from which this well-known song is taken, is founded on an old classic story. Campaspe, beloved of King Alexander, inspires an ardent passion in the breast of Apelles, whom the king had appointed to paint her portrait. Campaspe returns his love, and the monarch discovering their mutual treachery, resigns her to the artist. The fanciful little love-ditty is sung by Apelles as he works at his easel on the portrait of the beautiful Campaspe.

Page 40, 6th line from bottom. — *Rosalind's Madrigal.* This exquisite song from " Rosalynde ; Euphues' Golden Legacy," is more interesting when we remember that from this story Shakespeare was furnished with the material for that most delightful of his comedies, " As You Like It." The character of Shakespeare's arch, vivacious, yet love-tormented heroine, is suggested by this song. Lodge says in his preface to " Rosalynde : " " Room for a sailor and a soldier that gives you the fruit of his labor that he wrote on the ocean, when every line was wet with a surge, and every humorous passion counterchecked with a storm."

Page 47, line 14. — In " The Passionate Pilgrim," printed by William Jaggard in 1599, are found four stanzas of this madrigal with one of the answer called " The Milkmaid's Reply." In " England's Helicon " published in 1600, seven years after Marlowe's death, the poem appeared entire, and was ascribed to Marlowe. His " Jew of Malta," written some time previous to 1593, quotes two lines of it, and the first stanza occurs in " Merry Wives of Windsor " (act 3, scene 1). It is also quoted in Walton's " Complete Angler " with a stanza found neither in the " Passionate Pilgrim " nor the " England's Helicon." The following are the lines from Walton. They come in just before the last stanza : —

> "Thy silver dishes for thy meat,
> As precious as the gods do eat,
> Shall on an ivory table be
> Prepared each day for thee and me."

Page 47, line 17. — "England's Helicon" has this line thus : —
> "That valleys, groves, hills, and fields."

Page 52, line 1. — *Cupid's Ingratitude* is a paraphrase from an Ode of Anacreon, which seems to have been a favorite among the old poets, as I find several similar translations by different authors.

Page 61, line 5. — *More than light, perpetual bliss.* I have always been inclined to believe that this line should read ; "More than *life*, perpetual bliss," and that "*light*" is one of the numerous misprints which occur in the editions of the early dramatists. The sense of the stanza throughout is better sustained by the word *life*, and the next line, "Make me *live* by serving you," seems to make the reading more plausible. I make the suggestion with due reserve, as I have no one's opinion on the subject, and all editions read "*light*."

Page 64, line 15. — *The Triumph of Charis.* The first two stanzas of this song are to be found in "The Devil is an Ass," but the whole poem is included in Jonson's miscellaneous poetry.

Page 66, line 15 — The first stanza of this song is found in Shakespeare's "Measure for Measure." The entire poem was included in "The Passionate Pilgrim" and also in "The Bloody Brother," a tragedy by Beaumont and Fletcher. Its authorship has consequently been ascribed to the two poets, but not without dispute. I have always believed the stanza which is sung in "Measure for Measure" to be Shakespeare's own, and I find this opinion advanced and ably supported by R. G. White in his notes to "Measure for Measure," and in another work of his entitled "Shakespeare's Scholar."

Page 67, line 16. — This sonnet is from a collection called "Aurora; or, First Fancies of the Author's Youth," and is supposed to be the fruits of an unrequited passion, written about 1595, when the writer was fifteen years old.

Page 68, line 18. — *Go tell her through your chirping bills.* Does not this sweetest and delicatest of ancient love-songs bear a faint resemblance to "The Song of the Swallow" in Tennyson's "Princess"? To nothing less beautiful can it be compared. Excellent old Heywood — of whom no memorials are preserved except a few plays from over two hundred of which he was author — this little song enshrines his memory in everlasting fragrance.

Page 71, line 2. — The poem of " Cupid and Psyche," by Shakerly Marmion, is founded on the story in the Greek of Musæus. It has been a favorite, both with ancients and moderns. Among others, Thomas Heywood has written a play with the title " Love's Mistress," whose plot follows closely the old story. Shakerly Marmion is now almost unknown, but the poem from which these verses are taken is not altogether obscure, and deserves almost to rank with Marlowe's " Hero and Leander."

Page 80, line 8. — *The Reward of Innocent Love.* The collection called " Castara," from which these stanzas are taken, contains some most refined and beautiful poems. It is interesting to know that the heroine of Habington's verses was his wife. In those days, when marriage was always written of as a disenchantment, and the poet wrote sonnets only to his mistress, this picture of a pure connubial love is sweet and refreshing. His Castara was Lucy, daughter of Wm. Herbert, Earl of Powis.

Page 82, line 8. — *Sleaved silk.* I know only one other instance of poetry in which the word *sleave* occurs. That is in the celebrated line in Macbeth, " Sleep, that knits up the raveled *sleave* of care."

Page 90, line 9. — This epithalamium is found in the fifth sestiad of Marlowe's " Hero and Leander." The poem was left unfinished at Marlowe's death, and Chapman, who supplied the close of the poem, wrote this wedding hymn.

Page 93, line 1. — The play of the " Two Noble Kinsmen," from which this song is taken, is generally included among the works of Beaumont and Fletcher, and is one of the plays in whose composition Shakespeare is supposed to have been concerned. This song always impresses me as more Shakesperian than all the rest of the disputed drama. I do not find any song in Beaumont and Fletcher that has that simple, unaffected introduction of nature. The " ox-lips," and " primrose, first-born child of Ver," " all dear Nature's children sweet," even the " slanderous cuckoo," and " boding raven," are like Shakespeare, and remind one of the songs in " Love's Labor Lost," or Perdita's pretty enumerations of her floral gifts at the festival of the shepherds.

> " Daffodils,
> That come before the swallow dares and take
> The winds of March with beauty ; violets dim,
> But sweeter than the lids of Juno's eyes
> Or Cytherea's breath ; *pale primroses.*
> . . . . *bold oxlips* and
> The crown imperial."

Such flowers as these Shakespeare knew in his boyhood when he strolled through the woods and fields of Warwickshire.

Page 95, line 5. — This is part of a poem in "The Paradise of Dainty Devices." Its subject is an apothegm of Terence, " *Amantium iræ amoris redintegratia est.*"

Page 108, line 6. — There have always been diverse opinions as to the authorship of this poem, although it is now generally given to Richard Barnfield. Its history, as nearly as can be ascertained, is as follows : It first appeared in a volume by Richard Barnfield entitled " Lady Pecunia," which was printed in 1598 by John Jaggard. In 1599, William Jaggard, brother to John, printed a collection of poetry called " The Passionate Pilgrim," by William Shakespeare, in which the disputed song appears. In 1605 " Lady Pecunia " was reprinted without the poem, from which Collier concludes that John Jaggard first obtained it from William to swell Barnfield's small volume when first printed in 1598, and that it really was Shakespeare's. In " England's Helicon," published in 1600, the poem is given, ending at the line, " None alive will pity me," and signed *Ignoto*, a common signature of anonymous writers. In 1612 (according to Malone), William Jaggard published another edition of " The Passionate Pilgrim," in which was this poem, as well as a sonnet of Barnfield's, four stanzas of Marlowe's " Passionate Shepherd," " Take, O take those lips away," as it appears in Beaumont and Fletcher, and several songs by Thomas Heywood. Heywood quarreled with Jaggard for printing his verses, and insisted on a new title-page, which should not give the whole to Shakespeare. He declares that Shakespeare himself was offended at Jaggard " that he presumed to make so bold with his name." It seems not unlikely that the bookseller Jaggard had made the collection without much regard to authorship, and placed Shakespeare's name on the title-page as a valu-

12

able adjunct to its sale. It is certain that Heywood's poems were long afterwards included in editions of " The Passionate Pilgrim," and that Marlowe's poem and the two claimed by Barnfield are still printed in it.

It has also been a theory of one of the critics that this poem was formed of two distinct and separate ones, the first ending at the line, " None alive will pity me." I think this supposition must have arisen from the manner in which it is printed in " England's Helicon." There is no other evidence to warrant the theory. " England's Helicon," like other collections of the kind, frequently gave poems in a fragmentary state.

Page 111, line 8. — This "Ode to Melancholy" and the answer which follows, are often quoted as furnishing Milton with the suggestion for " Il Penseroso " and " L'Allegro."

Page 113, line 16. — This has been sometimes accredited to Dryden in modern collections of poetry.

Page 114, line 12. — This Labor Song, and the Lullaby which follows, are from the old play of " Patient Grissel," written by Dekker, Chettle, and Haughton. There can be little doubt as to the authorship of these songs. If they did not bear the undoubted impress of Dekker's style, it is plain that the Labor Song contains the same noble philosophy as the following lines from a play of which he was sole author : —

" Why should we grieve at want ?
 Say that the world made thee her minion, that
 Thy head lay on her lap, and that she danced thee
 Upon her wanton knee, she could but give thee a whole world,
 That's all, and that all's nothing. The world's greatest part
 Cannot fill up one corner of thy heart ;
 Were twenty kingdoms thine thou'd'st live in care,
 Thou could'st not sleep the better, nor live longer,
 Nor merrier be, nor healthfuller, nor stronger :
 If then thou wantest, make that want thy pleasure ;
 No man wants all things, nor has all in measure."

Page 116, line 1. — This grand old song is said to have been a great favorite with Charles II.

Page 125, line 2. — *Lament of Pythias.* The tragic play of " Damon and Pythias " is one of the oldest plays in the language. It is nearly contemporary with Sackville's "Ferrex and Porrex," the first English tragedy, and was prior to Whetstone's "Promos and Cassandra."

Page 143, line 3. — *Gammer Gurton's Needle* is the first English Comedy ever acted. It possesses a grotesque humor, which must have been much relished in its time. The panegyric on old sack is remarkable, apart from its real humor, for a dash and spirit in the verses, which is appropriate to the subject.

Page 155, line 3. — Middleton's play, "The Witch," is thought by many commentators to be older than Shakespeare's "Macbeth." The conjurations, "Come away, Come away," and "Black Spirits and Gray," which are in both plays, are much longer and fuller in Middleton's "Witch."

Page 162 line 4. — *With pictures full of wax and wool,* alluding to the images with which witches were said to represent the victims whom they wished to torment. The whole of this series of conjurations is interesting from the minuteness with which popular superstition and the traditional accounts of the rites of witchcraft is followed, as well as from a certain weird picturesqueness which the whole scene possesses. Jonson is erudite, even when he gives his imagination most play, and this masque is a learned picture of the orgies of these "secret, midnight hags."

INDEX OF AUTHORS.

———◆———

INDEX OF FIRST LINES.

www.ingramcontent.com/pod-product-compliance
Lightning Source LLC
Chambersburg PA
CBHW031057280326
41928CB00049B/960